Hilo Hattie

Hilo Hattie

A Legend in Our Time

a biography by
Milly Singletary

Mutual Publishing

Copyright © by Milly Singletary

All rights reserved. No part of this book may be reproduced in any form or by any electronic or mechanical means, including information storage and retrieval devices or systems, without prior written permission from the publisher, except that brief passages may be quoted for reviews.

Library of Congress Cataloging-in-Publication Data

Singletary, Milly, 1918-
Hilo Hattie, a legend in our time : a biography / by Milly Singletary.
p. cm.
Summary: "The story of Clara Inter, better known as Hilo Hattie, one of Hawaii's premier entertainers and ambassador of the aloha spirit"--Provided by publisher.
ISBN-13: 978-1-56647-780-2 (softcover : alk. paper)
ISBN-10: 1-56647-780-8 (softcover : alk. paper)
1. Hilo Hattie, 1901-1979. 2. Singers--Hawaii--Biography. I. Title.
ML420.H43S5 2006
782.42164092--dc22
[B]

2006019096

ISBN-10: 1-56647-780-8
ISBN-13: 978-1-56647-780-2

Design by Wanni

First Printing, September 2006
1 2 3 4 5 6 7 8 9

Mutual Publishing, LLC
1215 Center Street, Suite 210
Honolulu, Hawai'i 96816
Ph: 808-732-1709 / Fax: 808-734-4094
email: info@mutualpublishing.com
www.mutualpublishing.com

Printed in Taiwan

table of contents

list of photographs

chapter ten

No. 13 We sold lots of victory bonds in that Hotel St. Francis lobby. (Hannah Smith)

No. 14 Odetta and Kāhala Bray with me as we performed at the St. Francis—lots of times we'd go out and entertain servicemen. (Hannah Smith)

No. 15 The Red Cross was incredibly kind to me, and I did lots of shows for them. (Hannah Smith)

No. 16 I'd receive letter after letter of thanks. (Hannah Smith)

chapter eleven

No. 17 They loved it when Joe Keahiolalo and I did *Manuela Boy*. (Hawaiian Electric Company)

No. 18 June Shipstad broke her foot and I paid a visit. (June Shipstad)

chapter twelve

No. 19 Here we are cutting the wedding cake. (Carlyle Nelson)

chapter thirteen

No. 20 Gail and I enjoy some old-fashioned gabfests. (Gail Nelson)

No. 21 Gail comes to visit me after the stroke. (Gail Nelson)

chapter fourteen

No. 22 Holiday Inn gives us a grand welcome. (Carlyle Nelson)

No. 23 We often toured together. First row (left to right): Melanie, Lokelani, and Lei Aloha. Second row (left to right): Clara, the late Pineapple Pete, Carlyle, Danny Santos, and Chief Satini. (Carlyle Nelson)

chapter fifteen

No. 24 I enjoyed showing people how to make lei. (Hannah Smith)

No. 25 The ti leaves would arrive in gunny sacks. (Kāhala Bray Yancy)

No. 26 Kāhala and Leilani start stripping the leaves with a hairpin. (Kāhala Bray Yancy)

No. 27 Carefully check the length—never show the knees! (Kāhala Bray Yancy)

No. 28 Leaves are assembled, tied just to fit your waist. (Kāhala Bray Yancy)

chapter sixteen

No. 29 Clara with the Hawaiian Village Serenaders. (Carlyle Nelson)

No. 30 Danny wears the first jumpsuit in Hawaiʻi. (Irene Morton)

No. 31 Clara would do or say anything to make us laugh. (Lily Padeken Wai)

chapter seventeen

No. 32 Carlyle and I had so much fun playing at the 'Ilikai. (Carlyle Nelson)

No. 33 Arthur and I would close singing *Honey Come Back.* (Hawaii Tourist News)

No. 34 The Kailua Madrigal Singers are wonderful. (Halekūlani Hotel)

chapter eighteen

No. 35 Love that Hilo Hattie Paradise Cake. (Allan Hunt)

No. 36 Clara teaches visiting statesmen the hula. (Hawai'i State Archives)

chapter nineteen

No. 37 My first broadcast was with the *Harry Owens' Show.* (Carlyle Nelson)

No. 38 Just couldn't teach those birds to sing *The Cockeyed Mayor.* (KHET, Channel 11)

chapter twenty

No. 39 I crossed my eyes so many times doing *The Cockeyed Mayor* I went to a doctor to ask if my eyes might stay that way. He said it was the best exercise I could give my eyes. (Carlyle Nelson)

No. 40 From Hawaiian comedienne to a Japanese geisha for *Shinano Yoru.* (Lily Padeken Wai)

No. 41 Prince Kawohi and I used to do a comic hula on stage. One night his zipper broke and you should have seen him trying to do the hula with his legs together. (Bishop Museum)

No. 42 Then there was the night Colonel Sanders was in the audience. He too did a graceful hula. After we danced, I kissed him in appreciation. His comment? "If you teach me to do the hula, I'll teach you to cook chicken!" (*Honolulu Advertiser*)

No. 43 With the usual straw hat missing, Clara substitutes a lamp shade. (Lily Padeken Wai)

chapter twenty-one

No. 44 Lū'au need not to be as elaborate as this. It's the fun, merriment, music, singing, and dancing that make a lū'au. (Earl DeSilva)

chapter twenty-two

No. 45 Sometimes I just felt like sticking my tongue out at 'em. (Carlyle Nelson)

No. 46 Clara performs on a float in the Rosebowl Parade in California. (Bishop Museum)

chapter twenty-three

No. 47 For a moment Clara weeps when Webley Edwards presents the Nō Ka ʻOi (The Best) Award, then promptly starts doing the famous *Hilo Hattie Hop*. (March of Dimes)

chapter twenty-four

No. 48 Our quiet home in Kaʻaʻawa has the beautiful blue Pacific in the foreground and the beautiful green Koʻolaus in the background. (Carlyle Nelson)

No. 49 Of course, we're surrounded by tropical vegetation, flowers, and fruits. (Carlyle Nelson)

chapter twenty-five

No. 50 She's wonderful. (Carlyle Nelson)

chapter twenty-six

No. 51 Golf, needlepoint, making rugs—there are many sides to Clara's talents and she loves all pets. (Carlyle Nelson)

No. 52 Clara, herself a mastectomee, entertains at a fashion show with mastectomee models, and tells the mastectomen how important their attitude is. (Cancer Society)

No. 53 Clara Inter as Hilo Hattie performing the *Hilo Hop.* (Bishop Museum)

chapter twenty-seven

No. 54 The Aliʻi Float Hilo's Merrie Monarch Festival in 1971. (Jack Lord)

chapter twenty-eight

No. 55 Life is a funderful thing. (United Airlines, Jack O'Grady)

A great heartfelt thanks to the many who have shared so generously in relating their experiences in Clara's life, unanimously with a gigantic feeling of love for this gracious and humble lady. Since Clara's stroke left her unable to speak, it would have been impossible to authentically tell her story without these hundreds of friends, letters, diaries, working itineraries, and photographers so generously shared. Over 200 persons were interviewed—many on tape.

A giant thanks to Clara's husband, Carlyle Nelson, for his many patient interviews, for sharing scrapbooks, on-the-road itineraries, photographs, newspaper clippings, and other data without which this book could not have been written.

A giant thanks to my husband Fred, whose patience during these many months when all else was turned aside, shall forever be appreciated.

A giant thanks to editor and friend, Jeanne H. Brady, who adamantly refused to let me write "tho" for "though," or take any other shortcuts in the English language.

The first Kapi'olani maternity hospital was donated in 1890. (Kapi'olani Children's Medical Center)

chapter one

In the Beginning

She was born a pure Hawaiian at Kapi‘olani Maternity Home, Honolulu, on October 28, 1901, and christened Clarissa Haili. She danced and sang her way through life as Clara Inter, later to become internationally famous as HILO HATTIE. She brought laughter and happiness to millions, often ignoring the tragedies of her own life. This is HER story.

Clara's parents were divorced when she was born. “Mother was a practical nurse at the Kapi‘olani Maternity Hospital. We lived there till I was eight and I used to follow her from bed to bed when she made her rounds. It was so natural for me to cut up and kid. I learned a song about a pussy cat at the age of two-and-one-half and I used to sing it to the babies and their mothers.” During this time her older brothers and sisters were living with relatives.

In 1909, Clara's mother remarried and they moved from the hospital to Liliha Street. Although her parents were pure Hawaiian, the children were never allowed to speak the language. English was spoken at all times. It was the thing to do in those days. “I was twelve years old when I learned my first Hawaiian words while singing in the church choir. I learned to play that old organ too—you know—the one you pump.” In a reminiscent mood she continues, “Mother was very strict. I had many chores to do. Singing was OK, but dancing the hula was strictly kapu.”

In 1910, Clara's sister Thelma was born. Singing and dancing were such a natural part of her life that by the time Thelma was five,

Clara had taught her how to do the hula. On Saturdays, the old Bell Theater (where the Kukui Plaza now stands) would have amateur contests. From somewhere Clara rounded up a raffia skirt and a couple of lei and entered Thelma in the contest. Thelma won. Thelma recalls, "We were living on Archer Lane not far away. The prize was $5.00 and that was a lot of money in those days. We were afraid to tell mother. She was so strict. But we told her. At first she was angry, then she started to laugh and laugh saying, 'Well, guess it was alright.' She even let us keep fifty cents apiece. Clara and I were so close."

Clara's older brother, Harry, had learned to play the violin and the bass. When Clara was twelve, he was playing in the orchestra of the Bell Theater. A traveling vaudeville show came to town and Clara was just dying to see it. Finally, Harry agreed to slip her in on Saturday afternoon if she would do all his chores including cleaning all the lanterns—and wash all the dishes—he threw in for good measure. In recalling the incident later, Clara said, "I worked like the devil and went every week. That's where I learned the words to *Becky—I Ain't Coming Back No More.* Every Saturday I took my copy book and added more words and verses till I got it all."

1915 brought two big events—a trip to Hilo to sing with the church choir (her only trip to Hilo before she became famous as Hilo Hattie) and entrance to the Territorial Normal Training School to become a teacher.

"In 1917, my sophomore year, I had to leave school to help support the family. Mother was very ill. There was a sort of epidemic at that time. I got a job in the *Advertiser* Bindery at $3.00 a week." She stayed there for four years then returned to Normal School to complete her training. She graduated in 1923 and started teaching at the Waipahu Elementary School in September.

"During this time I met a very wise elderly man, John Keipe, who influenced my spiritual life greatly. Two visits from a *menehune* had changed his belief from money as God to a more personal God, and the founding of a religion, which he called *Ho'omana Na'auao.* The church at 710 Cooke Street he called *Kealaula oka Mālamalama*, and it was there I taught Sunday School, sang in the choir, and learned Hawaiian."

In the meantime, the strictness at home drove Clara into an early marriage at the age of eighteen. The license said "Age 20"; the date on the license was January 10, 1920. "Mother banned me from the house and told me never to darken their door again." Clara and John Baxter took up residence in the Kaka'ako district.

Thelma missed her sister terribly. "My sister Alice and I were attending the Sacred Hearts Convent on Fort Street. Clara's husband was in the Army. I missed her so much. One day after school I walked all the way to Kaka'ako just to see her. I got home late and mother wanted to know why. I lied. I told her I played late at school—but my sister told her I went to see Clara. I got a good whipping for that."

Thelma continues, "Then my mother got very sick. I asked Clara to come see her, but she would not. She said 'No, Mama told me never to come home.' Then Clara got sick and I told Mama. She went to see her and they were friendly from then on." That marriage was to be short lived and on July 2, 1926, Clara married Milton Douglas, also in the service—another short-term marriage. On April 16, 1930, Clara married Theodore Inter—a marriage that lasted until 1946.

But we're getting ahead of our story.

The faculty at Waipahu Elementary School in the early 1930s. (Mr. Jack Lindsey, Waipahu Cultural Center)

chapter two

Teaching School was an Inspiration

In 1923, Clara started teaching at the Waipahu Elementary School. Her first assignment was forty-seven first graders. Her First Class Teaching Certificate meant she could teach social studies, mathematics, English, reading, and art. She also taught music.

"We never knew from year to year where we would be assigned to teach. The School Board never notified us. They just sent notices to the newspapers then one day in the spring, usually May, all of these names would come out in the paper showing where we were assigned. They were arranged alphabetically, first by town, then by school, then by proper name. It was a mad house the day those notices came out in the paper. Everyone would be calling each other saying, 'Did you know you were assigned to Watertown, or some such school.' I was lucky. I was assigned to Waipahu Elementary every year."

Clara would play the piano while the class learned the words to *The Bells of St. Mary's* or *The Old Oaken Bucket*. Some of the students still recall the old Hawaiian songs she also taught. One student was quick to report, "She wasn't my home grade teacher, but we used to meet at noontime—kids from different grades—and she would teach us those beautiful Hawaiian songs. Every once in a while I hear one on the radio, but many of them are rarely played nowadays. We had such fun. Once in a while we'd go to other towns and compete in singing contests. We often won. Going to Honolulu in one of those plantation trucks was really a big event in those days."

Clara always put in that something extra. Carole Kamamura, another student, recalls those days as something that directed her life. She says, "Everybody loved her. Not only a nice teacher but a nice person—always gay. Never scolded anyone. She was my music teacher in the fifth, sixth, and eighth grades. She taught me to sing the Hawaiian Wedding Song, *Ke Kali Nei Au*. I'll never forget another song she taught us—*Lehua*. She made that song. I keep trying to find it. They have another song by that name, but it's not her song."

Carole continues, "I remember Hattie Boyle was another music teacher. One time we had this big production to put on in a theater. They called it a 'Fantasy.' Clara took care of all the songs and Hattie took care of all the dances. It was about flowers—roses, pansies, violets. We had paper costumes made like flowers. My brother was Old MacDonald and I was in the chorus. The audience loved it."

While the musical aspect became prominent because of her later fame, Clara was very much a serious teacher. First the students did their work, then, on Fridays, if they were good, she would sometimes treat them with a song and dance like the *Cockeyed Mayor*. Always, there seemed to be a roguish-impish-pixieish beam in her eyes. The children loved her. They still do. Back in October 1939, the Star Bulletin ran a special article by Eugene Burns with the heading, "KIDS SAY SCHOOL'S FUN IF HILO HATTIE TEACHES."

Student after student remembers Clara Inter, the teacher. After the trips to Portland for the teachers' convention and Los Angeles with the Shriners, many of them remember her as "Hilo Hattie," the teacher.

Time went on as Clara taught by day and danced by night. Although she was often requested to sing and dance at private parties, her professional career started in 1936 when she played the guitar and sang with the Royal Hawaiian Girls Glee Club. Clara chuckles, "We were a group of young wahine who just sang for the fun of it. We would get $25.00 and there were twenty-five of us, so we each got a dollar. On Saturday nights we would sing at the Royal Hawaiian and on Sunday nights we would sing at the old Wai'alae Country Club."

Though singing and dancing were fun, Clara never forgot her kids. She loved them. There were always extra events going on—singing contests, dancing contests (she taught her entire Brownie Scout Troup to do the hula!), gardening contests. Somewhere, Clara was always in the picture, whether a coach or a judge. She got her kids on radio too—like the broadcast on KGU, "A Plantation Girl Scout Writes to her Friend on the Mainland" and "Youth on Parade."

During a welfare drive in 1939, Clara promised to sing for every one of the twenty-four rooms in the school if they had a 100 percent participation and reached their goal. They MORE than reached their goal and Clara kept her promise, performing in every room. The students were thrilled. Many who saw her dance for the first time wrote notes of gratitude—"You dance nicely. You sing nicely, but you talk funny"; Clara often lapsed from pedantic English into pidgin, which delighted the students. "Thank you to dance for us." "I laughed and laughed till I almost couldn't stop." "You is very good teacher."

Although Clara was not a regular at the Kodak Hula Show, Ace Photographer "K. T." Tagawa's photos were so popular they were often used for publicity pictures. ("K.T." Tagawa)

chapter three

The Kodak Hula Show

In 1937, a young, energetic, and handsome guy by the name of Fritz Herman was managing Kodak Hawai'i, Ltd. Lots of people would come in the store saying, "Where can I get pictures of hula dancers?"

Remember, at that time "hula dancers" were thought of as a little "naughty."

"Hmmm," Fritz kept thinking, "That would be great publicity for Eastman Kodak." He had a brainstorm. Louise Silva, now known affectionately as Auntie Lou, was working as a secretary at the Inter-Island Steam Navigation Company. She also taught hula and had a group called The Royal Hawaiian Girls Glee Club performing at the Royal Hawaiian Hotel.

"I didn't even call her." I just went down to the office one morning and said, "Auntie Lou, would you let a few of your girls perform for me at the Queen's Beach one day a week?"

"What for?" She asked, "Nobody would come."

I kept insisting, "Let's give it a try!"

"Finally she gave in and on February 28, 1937, we had our first show with five musicians and four singers. There were no bleachers for those first shows. People would just sit on the grass. A group of Boy Scouts would form a circle around the performers so they wouldn't be disturbed by the audience. We only had forty or fifty people at those first shows."

It became a regular show beside the Waikīkī Natatorium, on the beach of Kapiʻolani Park. In 1969 a conflict arose about the Queen's Surf Restaurant at 2709 Kalākaua being on Government property. By that time, bleachers had been built at our show site, and many complained of it being an eyesore. After a two-year hassle, Mayor Frank Fasi won and the restaurant was demolished. The show was asked to vacate the property.

"We were lucky though," recalls Mr. Herman, "We were given permission to move the Show to our present location near the Shell."

Over a million people a year now see the show, which is performed every Tuesday, Wednesday, and Thursday. From approximately January through September, an extra show is given on Fridays. Although the show is not until 10 A.M., the gates open at 8:30 A.M. and there are always hundreds waiting to get a good seat. Often hundreds more are turned away, even though many sit on the grass after the bleachers are filled.

Clara Inter was never a regular on those shows because she was busy teaching school. She did, however, perform many times during the summers of 1937 through 1940, and often as a guest in later years. Her impact was so great a story of her life would be incomplete without a reference to the Kodak Hula Show—perhaps because several of her most publicized photographs were taken at that show by ace photographer "K.T." Tagawa.

Many of the beachboys of those days still remember Clara's performance with glee. Andy Kellikoa, a retired fireman who belonged to the Fireman's Hula Troupe back in the 1930s, remembers his days as a beachboy. "Sometimes I would climb the tree for the coconuts—you know, the one they do at the Kodak Show. In one of Clara's acts, she had a wooden horse sewn into a costume that made her look as though she were riding it. She called it *Kiele*. Sometimes I'd carry it from her car to the dressing room. That son of a gun was heavy! Sometimes when our Fireman's Troupe was performing at shows for public relations I would try to imitate her doing the *Cockeyed Mayor*. The people would always laugh—but no one can imitate Hilo Hattie. She's something special."

Clara's mythical horse, *Kiele*, performed with Clara at the Kodak Show and all over the country. (Carlyle Nelson)

Clara sends Don a picture saying thanks for the song. (Mrs. Don McDiarmid Sr.)

chapter four

How Hilo Hattie was Born

In 1936, Clara went to Portland, Oregon, with a teachers' convention. Naturally, there was entertainment aboard the ship and, naturally, Clara was part of it. Someone had a copy of Don McDiarmid's *When Hilo Hattie Does the Hilo Hop* and Clara did such a rendition of the song, the passengers went wild. Suddenly, Clara was Hilo Hattie.

After returning to Honolulu, she continued to do the number at private parties. At that time Clara was still very much the lady and graciously sang and played the guitar with the Royal Hawaiian Girls Glee Club.

One night, Auntie Lou, Clara, and Arthur Benaglia, manager of the Royal Hawaiian Hotel, were sitting along the wall watching the show. The comic hula dancer was performing, but not feeling well. Suddenly Arthur said, "Do you have anyone who can do that number?" "Sure, Clara could do it," Auntie Lou replied. Clara was shocked. "Me—I'm not going to get up in front of all those people and act like that." "Yes, you will." Auntie Lou was emphatic. "We are all part of a team. You work for me and you have to do what I say." Clara kept saying "No" and Auntie Lou kept saying "Yes" adding, "Someday you'll thank me for this." Under protest, Clara agreed to do a comic number.

Don McDiarmid was leading the band and Clara wanted him to let her do the *Hilo Hattie* number, but he was reluctant. In an article written by Don in the April 1947 issue of "Paradise of the Pacific," here's the way he tells it:

> Although I enjoy writing any type of song, my biggest thrills have come from creating mental personalities. It's fun to form a picture of a new song character and wait and see what finally happens. Sometimes the result is just what I'd expected.
>
> Aggie Auld, former hula darling of the Royal Hawaiian Hotel, was first to introduce "Little Brown Gal." She was all I had dreamed of, with her charm and grace, and beautiful long black hair. Kuʻu Lei also ran true to form as "South Sea Sadie," a character she has portrayed with much success in Hollywood. Napua Woodd was pleasantly surprising with her streamlined interpretation of the "Old Kamaʻāina from Lahaina," which she featured in the Hawaiian Room of New York's Lexington Hotel.
>
> But the greatest shock of all was the fate that befell my most popular brainchild, "Hilo Hattie," at the hands of Clara Inter. I had conjured up an exotic eyeful, tall and slender, voluptuous and glamorous. Well, if you've seen Clara in the role, I need say no more. She is neither tall nor slender, neither streamlined nor glamorous. But I hasten to add that Clara is doing all right for herself and for the song.

Doing all right indeed she was. Members of the band recall the first time she did the number at the Royal Hawaiian Hotel. They agree with a version of a story in an unidentifiable publication that reported the incident thusly:

> When Clara asked the conductor if she could do Hilo Hattie, he stared at her in disbelief. He grudgingly consented to play accompaniment for her, making no secret that he thought she wasn't the type for this song. Hattie, a charming person, is a bit buxom and not a glamour girl.
>
> Hilo Hattie's version of "Hilo Hattie" brought a tremendous ovation in the same place where the number

> had failed, and she had to make encore after encore. The amazed composer jumped from the bandstand, tears streaming down his face, as he confessed to Hattie he obviously had erred in visualizing a streamlined glamour girl for the song. "I never dreamed a character looking like you would put the number over," he admitted.

And that is how Hilo Hattie was born. Harry Owens helped make it legal in 1941, when Twentieth Century Fox insisted she use that name for the movie, *Song of the Islands*.

Performance after performance, she would fill her program with other songs. Invariably, someone in the audience would shout, "Do the *Hilo Hop*." Invariably, Clara would oblige, and invariably, the audience would roar with laughter. Many years later Clara sent Don a large picture autographed "Thanks for the song that made me."

Anytime the Shriners march, there's excitement in the air. (Shriners Hospital, Honolulu)

chapter five

The Shriners Turn Another Page of Excitement for Clara

1938 was filled with the same routine. Shows at the Royal Hawaiian and Moana Hotels, and Sunday nights at the Wai'alae Country Club. Teaching school during the day. It was also the year of the first parade honoring the pineapple industry. The Advertiser's Feb. 23 edition ran pages of pictures, headlined with "GIANT PARADE THRILLS THOUSANDS AS HO'OLAULEA FETE OPENS." Clara was there, bursting out now and then with *Manuela Boy*, which had just been released and was enjoying a great surge of popularity.

Then there were the many private parties and benefits. It seemed Clara never said no! "One of the biggest thrills I ever had in a benefit performance was the time Al Perry rented a sampan and took his whole group of Singing Surfriders and me over to Kalaupapa on the island of Moloka'i. For those of you who don't know, Kalaupapa is a leprosy settlement and the only place I know in the world where you actually can't spend a penny. By this time the disease, more commonly referred to in later years as Hansen's Disease, had been well contained and certainly none of the conditions existed as they did when Father Damien went there in 1873. Even today, tourists can only arrive by advance arrangements. They are then taken on a tour over the peninsula, given a brief history, and must leave the same day.

"We had been having a little feedback from our radio programs that the patients were really glued to their radios every time we went on the air. Al thought it would be a wonderful idea to go over and give a performance in person. As most of you know, I am quite famous for performing in my bare feet and this is the only occasion I can remember in my life where I performed in socks. No bare skin was allowed to touch the ground or buildings, including our feet while dancing. At first, we walked around the houses of the more serious cases that were not allowed to leave their buildings. House after house, they came out on the porches, applauding us enthusiastically. From there we performed in the auditorium and everyone who could walk or limp came to see us. They applauded like nothing we had ever heard before. It really gave us "chicken skin" (goose bumps). They were so thrilled and wanted to do something in appreciation—the only thing they could think of was to give us cans of salmon or corned beef—anything, as a gesture to show their appreciation. We really didn't want to take it but we knew the true feeling a Hawaiian has when he offers a gift, so we accepted."

Los Angeles was the scene of the Shriners' National Convention this year and Honolulu's Aloha Temple Shriners decided to take an entourage of Hawaiian entertainment to the event. The Shriners are fun-loving people and fun-loving entertainment was the order of the day. What could be more fun loving entertainment than the beloved Hilo Hattie? Clara Inter was first to be put on the request list, along with Al Kealoha Perry and his Singing Surfriders.

All life is a party to Hilo Hattie and this was about to be one of the biggest. On May 28, sixty-three Shriners, Hilo Hattie, and party marched down Fort Street behind the Royal Hawaiian Band to board the *S.S. Matsonia* for Los Angeles. The first night out the menu read like this:

Menu

Celery Hearts   Salted Nuts   Olives

Fresh Crab Flake Cocktail

Consommé Fatima

Hawaiian Frog Legs Sauté, Meuniere

Filet Mignon, Stuffed Tomatoes, Fresh Asparagus Tips
Croquette Potatoes

Golden Pheasant, Juniper berry Gravy, Red Currant Jelly
Bread Sauce

Fountainbleu Salad

Aloha Temple Delight

Roquefort Cheese

Coffee

"I nudged Al," saying—"Eh, where's the rice and poi? Hawaiian frog legs?? My 'ōpū was really stuffed that night."

The entourage included dancers Emmaline Souza, Lillian Du Pont, Lila Guerrero, and Marguere Mahi, along with Clara. The Singing Surfriders led by Al K. Perry, included Simeon Bright, Robert Kauahikaua, David Kelii, Andrew Bright Jr., and Frank Cockett.

What a reception they received in San Pedro! Planes soared overhead, dipping their wings. Yachts and small craft in the harbor all joined in the gala celebration. Newsmen climbed aboard and the papers were flooded with pictures of them.

With a reception like that, what could you do but strike up the band and start doing the hula? And that's what they did—right at dockside. Sheriff Biscailuz was one of the Shriners' delegates that went down to meet them and he got in the mood mighty quick, doing the hula right with them. Later, pictures in the newspaper showed him doing the same thing when the Hawaiian group met in his office at City Hall.

First thing on the agenda was a gigantic parade through downtown Los Angeles. A giant lei had been put up in their honor and they marched down Broadway, all joining hands and singing. Traffic was stopped—even streetcars couldn't run! At Seventh and Broadway several restaurants started serving breakfast in the street—ham and eggs, wheat cakes, and coffee. It was a riot in a nice sense.

Sometimes FUN can get a little out of hand. The popularity of the open house reception the Aloha Temple put on at the Biltmore Hotel got that way. The stream of visitors was so heavy, guests had to be put on a timetable, allowing approximately twenty minutes to each. Entering through the front door, guests sipped Hawaiian punch, listened to Hawaiian music, and watched the hula being danced—then were politely (if that's possible) ushered out the back door through the kitchen, as more kept flocking in the front door.

"The actual convention was on June 7, 8, and 9 and we had arrived on the third. We sure spread the aloha spirit around those next couple of days. We danced in the Biltmore lobby; we danced in front of City Hall and in City Hall. It was great.

"Although we didn't attend several of the meetings of the convention, there were many spectacular events we did attend. The first official event was vesper services held in the Hollywood Bowl, with branches of Shriners from every state taking part in the ceremony. There were horse shows and parades and all kinds of exciting things. The last night of the convention was sensational with floats and displays from every major studio in Hollywood, all in the Memorial Coliseum. Harold Lloyd was chief rabbi of Al Malaikah temple and was in charge of this event, which they called a "Motion Picture Electrical Pageant."

"We did a few nights of entertainment while we were there—a couple of nights at Ciro's and the Mocambo. Occasionally, there was a private party that wanted us. One particular night that stands out in my mind was a birthday party for Mrs. Fogelson from Texas. They had hired the entire House of Murphy for the evening and had it all decorated Hawaiian style. They called it a lūʻau, but it wasn't like the kind we have at home. Al and his Singing Surfriders played music all evening and I did eight or nine numbers.

"Next month we returned to Honolulu on the *Lurline* and were delighted to see those grass skirted girls of the Royal Hawaiian Girls Glee Club on the dock to greet us. Don McDiarmid had planned a special welcome party at the Royal Hawaiian Hotel and then Sunday night another party at the Wai'alae Country Club with Joe Ikeole's band."

Then things went back to normal. Dancing by night and teaching by day. Always those extra events like giving badges to Boy Scouts and a trip to Moloka'i in November for a Kaunakakai PTA benefit.

We sail on the *S.S. Matsonia* for Los Angeles, then by plane to New York. (Lily Padeken Wai)

chapter six

Time Out for the St. Regis Hotel in New York

1939 was a great year:

- My sister Thelma won the Hawaiian Women's Tennis Championship.
- I was thrilled to entertain at Washington Place for Governor Poindexter.
- The Royal Hawaiian celebrated its twelfth birthday with an extravaganza of sixty-five entertainers. ʻIolani Luahine, Lila Guerrero, Auggie Auld, and Mapuana Bishaw all did solos. There was, oh, so much entertainment and dancing—groups like Bray's Aloha Serenaders, The Royal Hawaiian Girls Glee Club, The Beamer Troupe, Joe Ikelole's Hawaiians, and Bill Smith's Islanders. Of course I got to dance too!
- It was the year the Haleʻiwa Hotel reopened on the North Shore, and what a gala event that was. People came from Wahiawā, Kahuku, Pearl City—all over. Most of the guests arrived by special train, and that ride in itself was quite a party. Al Perry's Singing Surfriders provided the music. The Haleʻiwa bridge was all covered with ti leaves and the hotel was a mass of beautiful flowers. I did a few impromptu numbers that night that caused a riot of laughter. I just felt so good.
- The *Star Bulletin* held its annual garden contest and I was asked to be a judge at the ʻAiea School.
- Lei Day was also celebrating its twelfth anniversary and this

year's celebration was as great as ever. Edean Ross was crowned Queen by Mayor Crane. The University of Hawai'i's amphitheater was jammed. Al Perry's Singing Surfriders played and people from all the Islands made a special presentation. My greatest fun was getting Don Blanding (creator of Lei Day) to come up and do the hula with me.

- My sixty singing-strong chorus at the Waipahu Elementary School won first place in the three school concerts put on in June. Those hours of practice on *He Nohea 'Oe* and *Leilehua* showed their reward.
- The Rotary Club of Waikīkī held its charter meeting on June 20, at the Green Lantern Restaurant. I was honored to be asked to entertain at that first meeting.
- Of course I was still teaching by day, dancing by night and doing the Kodak Hula Show during the summer.
- My greatest thrill was being invited to entertain at a new Hawaiian Room in the St. Regis Hotel in New York. I asked for a leave of absence from my teaching job and was so happy when it was granted.

Vincent Astor was a frequent visitor to the Islands in the late 1930s. Sometimes he came on his yacht, *Nourmahal*, sometimes by ship, always staying at the Royal and always enjoying the Garden Terrace entertainment. He loved Hawai'i so much and wanted to capture that mood in his St. Regis Hotel.

At that time the St. Regis already had three entertainment centers: the Maisonette Russe, the Iridium Room, a very popular night spot with its disappearing ice skating rink, and the ever popular St. Regis Roof Garden. He decided to remodel the Maisonette Russe into a Hawaiian Room.

By this year regular air service was flying to Hawai'i, and Gaston Lauryssen, General Manager of the St. Regis, was flown to Honolulu to register his impressions and make arrangements to hire entertainers. One thing for sure—Hilo Hattie was going to be part of the show and Elmer Lee, known in the inner circles as Hawai'i's most in-demand high society orchestra, was included. Lily Padeken, one of the top hula dancers, was also in popular demand at Mr. Lee's parties, so she, too, was included. Other entertainers hired to complete the group included

Leo Lani and Mapuana Bishaw. Elmer Lee's quintet included Lee, Renny Brooks, Arthur Māhoe, Sam Kapu, and Eddie Kinalau.

Mr. Astor left no stone unturned to assure that this room, to be called the Hawaiian Maisonette, would really capture the mood of the Islands.

"We left Honolulu on Friday, September 15, on the *Matsonia*, then flew to New York as the new room was scheduled to open on the twenty-eighth. Actually, we landed at Newark then motored to New York through the Holland Tunnel. That was a thrilling experience. Fortunately, the opening was delayed until October. We needed that time to get oriented, find a place to stay and get used to our new setting.

We stayed at a small hotel around the corner from the St. Regis. Things got pretty much down to a routine before long. The show was a great hit and the room was crowded every night. At the same time, Ray Kinney and his orchestra were playing at the Lexington Hotel. Once in a while, we would go see their show. We played two shows a night and had Monday off.

"I enjoyed those double decker buses and sometimes I'd just go for a ride without knowing where I was going. We did get to see the World's Fair, the Bronx Zoo, Statue of Liberty, and the Empire State Building. One time I took a "mini" vacation and went to Washington, D.C. Even went to a concert at Carnegie Hall. The weather was getting cold and all of us bought some woolen clothing.

"One night after the show, Leo Lani had a date with her boyfriend who had a car. She thought it would be a great idea to take off after the show and drive to Niagara Falls. Lily and I had heard so much about Niagara Falls; we were thrilled to have Leo invite us to go along. It was snowing a little as we left New York City and the further we drove the worse the storm got. The heater in front kept Leo and her boyfriend sort of warm, but Lily and I were freezing in the back seat. We were out in farming country and would stop to ask directions the few times we saw a light burning. We even had a flat tire. Some farmers helped us and told us to go back home—that we weren't prepared to drive in this kind of weather. By the time morning came, the winds were blowing the snow so hard we couldn't see the road—it was horrifying. I don't think we made more than two miles an hour, but we finally got back to our hotel.

"A few times we played at private parties. One time the boys and I did one at Doris Duke's home. The union found out about it and forbade the boys to take their gear from the hotel after that. Twice we put on a special performance at the St. Regis Roof—both private parties for debutante balls.

"It was wonderful having Lily for a roommate. She was only nineteen and this was her first experience away from home. She was like a daughter, as well as a friend, 'cause she was always willing to venture into new places.

"I was given two tickets to the Army-Navy game in Philadelphia, so we bundled into our heavy clothes and our fur-lined galoshes and took a train to Philadelphia to see the game. It was a great experience, but we were late getting back for the show. The girls knew where we had gone, but I hadn't told Elmer. Anyway, the girls filled in a number for us and we quickly slipped out of our heavy clothing and were out on the stage within ten minutes, just as though nothing had happened.

"It certainly was a different routine from our life in Hawai'i. The show didn't get out till about 2 A.M. Then we'd often go some place for a cup of coffee and chat till about 4 A.M. By the time we got home and ready for bed, it was usually five or six in the morning so we'd sleep till four or five in the afternoon. Then we'd go out for dinner, or breakfast, or whatever you want to call it.

"There was a Horn & Hardart Automat around the corner from our hotel. I got a kick out of eating there. It was like nothing I had ever seen before. It looked like a wall of post office boxes with glass doors and you would put in a nickle or a dime, open the door, and pull out your food. If you were really hungry, you could go back four or five times and do the same thing. There was such an assortment to choose from.

"We continued the show until February when we decided it was time to come home. New York was too cold and too fast. Lily and I flew back across the country, boarded the *Lurline* and returned to wonderful, sunny Hawai'i.

Clara and her contagious smile. (Carlyle Nelson)

What a welcome of lei! (Carlyle Nelson)

chapter seven

Welcome Home Clara

On February 21, 1940, the *Lurline* steamed into Honolulu Harbor with homesick Hilo Hattie and two hula dancers, Lily Padeken and Leo Lani. There were other celebrities aboard too, like George Brent and Ralph Forbes, but none got the welcome bestowed on Clara. There were tons of lei—ginger, plumeria, roses, pīkake—they were all there, burying her up to her eyes.

There were tears in her eyes. She was glad to be home. "Too cold and too fast," she reported.

Full pages of ads screamed "WELCOME HOME CLARA." KGMB sent a greeting via an ad that read "Aloha Nui Loa to Clara Inter, Singing Star of the Maxwell House Party, Hawai'i Calls, and other radio broadcasts." Ray Kinney's ad read "Aloha to a Real Trouper, Clara Inter. Hawai'i is Hawai'i again. Clara's home! Only a real trouper could have been missed so much and so sincerely.... Only a real artist and a friend could have made so great an impression." Al Kealoha Perry and his singing Surfriders ran a big ad to "Bid Aloha to our own Clara (Hilo Hattie) Inter" and announced a big aloha party at the Wai'alae Saturday night. Joseph Ikeole's ad read "Aloha Clara Inter. Hawai'i's favorite daughter, dancer, singer, wit, and an all-around good fellow." There were many more.

Perhaps the real point is missed in all of the above for, in addition to a sincere aloha spirited welcome home, these ads were inviting all her friends to two large parties to be held in her honor—one at the Wai'alae and the other at the Royal.

The Wai'alae Golf Club even printed a special menu. It had Clara's picture on the front and inside was a picture of Al Perry's Surfriders including Mystery Cockett, David Kelii, Simeon Bright, Squeeze Kamana, Andrew Bright, Bob Kauahikaua, and Bill Akamahou.

The menu was especially adapted for Clara's pidgin English.

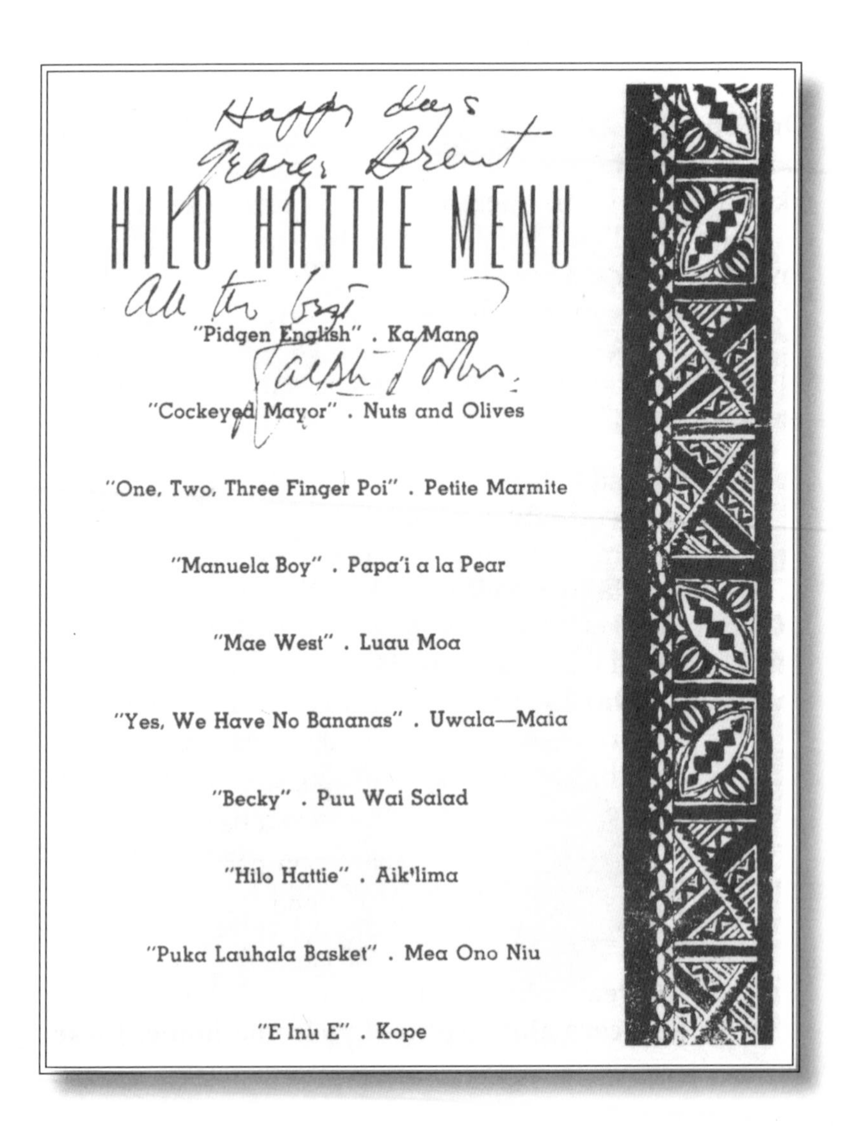

HILO HATTIE MENU

"Pidgen English" . Ka Mano

"Cockeyed Mayor" . Nuts and Olives

"One, Two, Three Finger Poi" . Petite Marmite

"Manuela Boy" . Papa'i a la Pear

"Mae West" . Luau Moa

"Yes, We Have No Bananas" . Uwala—Maia

"Becky" . Puu Wai Salad

"Hilo Hattie" . Aik'lima

"Puka Lauhala Basket" . Mea Ono Niu

"E Inu E" . Kope

Clara continued performing and teaching until 1940 when things came to a climax. The Board of Education gave her a choice of "dancing or teaching." Each year it was necessary for teachers to get approval to carry on outside jobs and each year Clara received her official permission with no problems.

According to Territorial Law a teacher could not hold another job if it deprived another person of a job and, supposedly, there were teachers out of work. Someone made Clara a test case. In October of 1940 she decided to give up teaching and enroll in the University of Hawai'i to work towards her B.E. degree. "After all, I can make more money singing and dancing than I can by teaching and I can earn my degree at the same time." It wasn't quite that simple though. Clara did a lot of soul searching, wondering which way to go. She really loved both careers and oftentimes she was quoted as saying, "I'll be a school teacher long after they've forgotten Hilo Hattie."

A conference with Dean Wist of the University cinched it. "There's going to be a war and keeping up morale is very essential. We can always get a new teacher, but there's only one Hilo Hattie."

The papers were full of headlines: "Department of Education Gave Choice Of Dancing And Singing Or Teaching"; "Hilo Hattie Does A New Kind Of Hop"; "Quits Teaching, Returns To School"; "Hattie And Her Hula Get Higher Education."

And another page in the life of Clara Inter was turned.

It all started at the Royal Hawaiian Hotel. (Hawai'i State Archives)

chapter eight

Harry Owens Enters Clara's Life and Her World Changes

No better account of Harry Owens' triumphant return to Hawai'i and the Royal Hawaiian Hotel in September of 1940 could be written than his own version as described in his autobiography, "SWEET LEILANI, The Story Behind the Song" (published by Hula House, P.O. Box 5454, Eugene, Ore. 97405). With the kind permission of Harry O., Chapter 40, which outlines Harry's first encounter with Clara, opens like this:

> As sweet and fine a soul as ever breathed the pure Hawaiian air, possessing a heart of gold, the spirituality of an angel, the knowledge and understanding of an Island priestess, this is a partial description of Hawai'i's first lady.
>
> And fully realizing the inadequacy of my description, I hasten to add: She's a devil-may-care pixie, a happy, laughing, talented, funny-wonderful wahine.
>
> You will question: "All of these attributes in a native Hawaiian comedienne?"
>
> My answer is immediate: "Aye, all these and more."
>
> Many are the plagiaristic sparrows who have pecked away in an attempt to imitate her. But this they do no more. Her Hawaiian brothers have an expression which

sums up the utter futility of trying to impersonate her, "Waste time"!

The mold that fashioned her viewed the pattern it had created and wisely decreed: "No more now. This is the masterpiece. There can be only one."

Long ago she became known as my adopted daughter. Actually Hilo Hattie is a year my senior, so that makes her, let us say, younger than springtime.

On that night when first our paths crossed, she was not yet Hilo Hattie. She was Clara Haili Inter…, one of forty chubby fun-loving, singing-dancing wahine, who with their leader, Louise Akeo, comprised what was known as "The Royal Hawaiian Girls Glee Club"….

Harry goes on to describe the fantastic Homecoming Party. 'After playing an hour for dancing—Mr. Benaglia, manager of the Royal, came to the bandstand and took over. The whole group was escorted to a ringside table. Harry, hardly able to see over the myriad of lei around his neck, was accepting handshakes by the hundreds. Champagne flowed, the lights went dim, and a show of over a hundred of Hawai'i's finest entertainers performed…

Finally the piece de resistance: Louise Akeo and her Royal Hawaiian Girls Glee Club, those forty happy, chubby, wahine. How wonderful they were! They sang the old songs, the new songs, the sad songs, the happy songs.

I had known Louise since my first days in Hawai'i—had worked with her. But who, I wondered, is that delightful, full-of-fun-pixie—front row, fourth from the left? She was new to me. And she never stopped enjoying herself. In serious songs, spiritual songs, whatever, she performed for the sheer love of it. She swished with a coquettish gyration, a sort of hula-hop, which completely intrigued me. Have to meet that wahine!…

At the show's conclusion, Freddie took over and the Royal Hawaiians played again for dancing.

I sought out Louise Akeo. "Who is that little menehune, Luika—you know, the fourth from..."

"That's Clara, Papa-san," interrupted Louise. "Want to meet her?"

And that's how and when I met the five-foot-two, devil-may-care, funny-wonderful wahine—Clara Haili Inter.

Next day Clara lunched with me and we talked of many things. Her sweetness came through; her University of Hawai'i English was impeccable. And she could switch from it to the most irresistible "pidgin." Delightful!

"Clara," I asked, "how did you happen to dream up that very cute 'hop-business'?"

"Oh, that happened," she replied, "when I was working out a hula for 'Hilo Hattie.' Do you know the song?"

"Indeed I do. Don McDiarmid wrote it three or four years back, when he was playing trumpet for me." I added: "It's a real cute number. I'd like to see you do it."

"When, Papa-san?"

"Oh, say at rehearsal tomorrow?"

"Maika'i, fine," said Clara Haili Inter, "can do."

A few days later, I phoned Louise Akeo.

"Luika," I began, "please promise not to hate me."

"I could never hate you Papa-san. What's your pilikia?"

"I'm a thief, Luika. I'm about to steal one of your girls."

"I knew it was coming," Luika replied. "Clara is too talented, Papa-san, to go on forever as one of forty girls. It had to happen."

"You're not mad at me then?"

"No huhū, Papa-san."

"Luika, I love you."

"Mahalo, Papa-san."

"...Within a week she premiered with me at the Royal

> Hawaiian. It was a Saturday night. The courtyard was packed. Her success was instantaneous. A year later we changed her professional name to Hilo Hattie. It was done in legal fashion, in a Los Angeles court…
>
> With that Saturday night premiere, there began an association which lasted until the day of my retirement, many years later."

There will be many references to Hilo Hattie's career as it evolved with Harry Owens, but I thought the above account of their meeting was marvelous.

I always had a good time kidding around. (Hannah Smith)

I made my first movie this year—*Song of the Islands.* (Hannah Smith)

chapter nine

1941—The Trip to Los Angeles

"1941 brought a new kind of experience in my life. For the first time since 1923 I wasn't teaching my kids and I missed them. Instead, I was taking classes at the University of Hawai'i and, fortunately, still performing at nights. We did a lot of benefits as usual. Several times there were pictures in the papers when I had a group of sailors lined up to learn the hula. We had those dances in the pavilion at Ala Moana Park for the whole fleet. Often I went out and entertained on the ships. Sometimes I get the years a little mixed up, but I do remember going from one carrier to another, crawling up and down the rope ladders, just like the sailors.

"June, though, was the biggest turning point in my life that year. Harry Owens called from Los Angeles, offering me a two-week contract at the Paramount Theater. He hinted it might be extended and there might be a part for me in a movie with Betty Grable and Jack Oakie. When he offered to cable round trip fare—that did it. He also said he needed a couple good musicians like Fred Tavares and Danny Stewart, and a couple good hula dancers. He offered to pay the fare for all of us, and in June we left on the *Lurline* for Los Angeles.

"The Paramount job was interesting. We did a stage show alternating with the movie, *One Night in Lisbon*, with Fred McMurray. Our contract was extended another two weeks. While working at the Paramount, I received a contract to do a small part in the movie, *Song of the Islands*, as Harry had hinted.

"You should have seen my eyes the first time I reported to work for Twentieth Century-Fox. They told me to go to Stage 14. When I walked in that door, I was flabbergasted. The ceiling was at least seventy feet tall—it was a tropical paradise everywhere. There were giant palm trees, Hawaiian fern, hibiscus, bougainvillea, plumeria—a huge waterfall—even a giant banyan tree that covered half the stage—and the stage covered over two acres. The floor was completely covered with sand—tons of it—with some sod placed in special areas. The background was a huge mural that several artists had painted. It looked so natural I forgot myself one time and walked right into it. Someone said it covered 10,000 square feet. I didn't know how much 10,000 square feet was, but it looked just as though I was looking at my beloved Hawai'i.

"I was soon pulled away from this magical scene and told to report to the Makeup Department. There the makeup artist created a new face, which made me feel uncomfortable. When I reported back to the working stage, the Director threw his hands in the air and yelled, 'Take it off.' He was only referring to the makeup, of course. I was glad. From then on all I ever used was a touch of eyebrow pencil and lipstick."

"It was strange those first few days. I wasn't important, but had to be on the set anyway. Betty Grable, Jack Oakie, and Victor Mature were the stars. She is so beautiful, I thought as I was watching her. They're paying me to watch this? Then, of course, they would shoot a scene including me. It seemed like such a simple scene, and yet they would shoot it over and over.

"One of the most memorable scenes was the giant lū'au. It took place in front of the waterfall. They had prepared tons of food. Someone told me they had six whole roasted pigs, thirty chickens, 500 coconuts, 100 pounds of fish, 10 dozen pineapples—and best of all—150 pounds of poi! Somehow word had gotten around the set that the entire crew was going to be invited to share the food after the final shot was taken. There were over a hundred Polynesian extras on the set and, for awhile there, I forgot I was in Hollywood. I managed to stick my finger in the poi a couple of times during the shooting. They took the shot at least six times—then somebody shouted, 'Everybody eat!'—and it looked like King Kamehameha coming over the Pali. People came out from everywhere. Within an hour the food was gone and there was nothing left but messes of bones, banana peelings, coconut shells—all kinds of debris. It was really quite a lū'au.

"After the Paramount contract was over, Harry got another job at the Hotel Miramar in Santa Monica. We played outdoors by the pool area. All the palm trees and balmy breezes sort of reminded me of home. From there we went to the Blossom Room of the Roosevelt Hotel on Hollywood Boulevard.

"Performing at night, making movies during the day, along with a few recordings, was getting to be a heavy routine. Harry was feeling the pressure too. His contract with *Song of the Islands* called for writing all the songs in the picture.

"One day we had a meeting and discussed the rush, rush of Mainland life. All of a sudden I suggested we split our entertaining time between the Mainland and Hawai'i, suggesting that New Year's at the Royal Hawaiian Hotel would be wonderful. Papa-san thought it was a wonderful idea and said he'd cable the hotel immediately. Within an hour a return cable read:

YOU OPEN NEW YEAR'S EVE.
WE'LL WELCOME YOU HOME.

"Harry's contract at the Roosevelt Hotel ran until the middle of December, so everything worked out just great. I was so excited about going home.

"Then came December 7, 1941. Over the radio came the shattering news, 'The Japanese have bombed Pearl Harbor.' I was alone in my apartment and sat there stunned. Then I jumped in my car and went over to see Harry and Bess. They, too, were in shock. The next few days we seemed to walk around in a daze. We continued playing at the Hotel Roosevelt, but Papa-san was very restricted in the songs he could play and what he could say. He finally got so disgusted, he cancelled the whole thing and went on a vacation. Even now, I don't like to think about those days."

We sold lots of victory bonds in that Hotel St. Francis lobby. (Hannah Smith)

1942—San Francisco During the War Years

During the next few months Clara did a lot of traveling—mostly singles up and down the West Coast—occasionally, a week here or there. Clara was back in Los Angeles one June morning when she received a call from Harry Owens. Dan London had called Harry from San Francisco and wanted the whole gang to do a show in the Mural Room of the St. Francis Hotel. Harry was so excited, he reported the conversation in detail.

"The place is jumpin,'" said Dan. "You can't believe it until you see it. And they're screaming for entertainment. This is where you belong, Harry. And right now! You and your music, plus Hilo Hattie and the hula girls—nobody could ask for a better send off."

"How about the radio-broadcasting situation?" Harry asked. "At the Blossom Room they gagged me. Can I be myself on the air?"

"Positively yes," Dan replied. "There will be no restrictions. None whatsoever."

"Fine, I'll open. How about next Tuesday?"

"Great. I'll have your suite ready."

Needless to say, Clara was thrilled with the prospect of the whole troupe getting together again with a regular show at the St. Francis Hotel. "Wowie—those one nighters can get tiresome.

"Harry started contacting the band and I started thinking about the hula dancers. I thought about the Bray sisters immediately. They had worked with Harry many times before, and what fine dancers they were! By this time, both were married and, fortunately, still living in the Los Angeles area. The Bray name was so famous in the entertainment field people always referred to them as Odetta Bray Rosson and Kāhala Bray Yancy. I called both of them immediately. They both said 'yes.'

"Kāhala and her husband wanted to drive to San Francisco in their own car. The next morning, Harry picked me up and we went over to the Rossons. They were living in a great big house on Haskell Avenue in Encino, with maid and all. They fixed a huge breakfast for us, then we jumped in Harry's car and headed for San Francisco—singing all the way. We were so excited we drove straight through and checked in the St. Francis that night.

"Working at the St. Francis was fun. We performed in the Mural Room nightly, plus tea dances on Saturday afternoons. I was very impressed. They had converted the bandstand sorta like a grass shack. The dance floor was sunken, and all over the room there were huge mirrored pillars—on the walls, floor to ceiling murals of San Francisco in early days. Now it's all lobby where the Mural Room used to be, and the murals are gone. I understand they couldn't save any of them. Even though they had been painted on canvas, as hard as they tried, the canvas tore.

"The room was jammed every night. In fact, all San Francisco seemed jammed. We did a lot of rehearsing those first few days, but before long, I found my way to Chinatown, only a few blocks away, to try out some new restaurants. They were good. I think I tried eight or nine during the next few weeks until I found a favorite. There's nothing like a huge bowl of steaming won ton mein to brighten the spirits in chilly San Francisco. Sometimes, I think I rated Chinese restaurants by the number of won ton they put in the soup.

"In the lobby they sold Victory Bonds. Lots of times, I sat in the lobby stringing lei. At other times, we would put on a show. Naturally, the hotel lobby was crowded with servicemen and those servicemen always seemed to get such a kick out of taking a free hula lesson.

"We hadn't been in San Francisco a month until requests started coming in for benefits and charity shows. On my own, I used

Odetta and Kāhala Bray with me as we performed at the St.Francis—lots of times we'd go out and entertain servicemen. (Hannah Smith)

to go down to the dock every time I heard a ship was coming in from Hawai'i. There were mothers and children who had been evacuated from Hawai'i. Naturally, they would feel strained and it seemed to cheer them up when someone from their own Aloha-land would greet them with a few words. Sometimes, I'd entertain from the dock. Sometimes, they'd allow me to go aboard ship. Oftentimes wounded servicemen were coming back from the war. I did my job. Every night I performed on cue, but my heart sang best when I was making those unhappy souls smile.

Some of the women of San Francisco baked cookies to give to the servicemen at USO shows and Red Cross dances. The military decided it was confusing with too many people getting involved, so they asked the volunteers to work through the Red Cross. That was the time the Red Cross formed a section they called the Cookie Brigade. Mrs. William Roth was one of those volunteers and she remembers:

The Red Cross was incredibly kind to me, and I did lots of shows for them. (Hannah Smith)

"Clara was always willing to go. Often we would go out to secret places with just a few men stationed there; sometimes, it would be in a place all closed in and down under the ground. I remember the time Clara thought the men wouldn't be able to see her perform because it was so crowded—so she jumped up on the ping-pong table and did the hula. The guys clapped and clapped."

"The Red Cross was incredibly kind to me. Of course, I did a tremendous number of shows for them. Time after time, I got letters of appreciation like the one on the page 49.

"They invited me everywhere, and sometimes I think I went everywhere."

Clara remembered some of those war incidents too. "Sometimes Kāhala and I would go out on a truck and just the two of us would perform. We had a little record player with us and my uke. The Sergeant would blow a whistle, and those guys would come out from everywhere.

"It was a beautiful year. But it was a sad year."

Clara was living at the St. Francis Hotel. "We weren't allowed to do any cooking in our room, but I had a hot plate anyway. Sometimes, I felt it necessary to get away from the crowds, open a can of soup, and sit down and write some letters. We had maid service, but I always greeted them at the door when they were handing out fresh linens. I'd do all my own cleaning. They understood. Sometimes, they'd even come in and we'd sit down and chat."

The Mural Room made a lot of people happy in those days. Clara was amused at an article in one of the local papers—so amused, she clipped it. The article read like this:

> Keep 'em rolling under the tables is the jolly slogan of Hilo Hattie, who clowns through dances and songs, capers around on the weirdest horse that ever galloped in a ballroom and, in general, keeps the Mural Room in a whirl of merriment. She's the hectic feature of Harry Owens' orchestra, which is entering its third month at the St. Francis, an engagement any band could dangle at its belt as a trophy.

Harry Owens and Hilo Hattie played the same routine, usually twenty-six weeks of the year. Then they'd go on the road for a few months, and always a couple months of vacation.

"In 1943, we went back to the St. Francis again. This time we wound up our contract on New Year's Eve. What a bash that was. Harry had invited the whole band and a lot of the hotel crew up to his suite for a rousing greeting of the New Year. It must have been three o'clock by the time everyone got there. Bobby Nielsen was head maitre d' at that time and he always fixed special buffets for Harry. That night there was champagne and beer, caviar and cold cuts, sandwiches and soda pop." The band remembers Clara gathering them all together so they could march in in force. "I remember we couldn't all get in one, or even two, elevators, so Clara told us to wait when we arrived at Harry's floor—until we all were there. Then Clara marched down the aisle and we all followed her, singing *Auld Lang Syne*."

"We spent many more happy years at the Mural Room in San Francisco. Sometimes, Harry would call a meeting in the middle of the day." Vern Sellin recalled, "We always knew whether it was going to be lengthy, because Harry always called his meetings saying, 'It's gonna be a one-bottle meeting' or, 'a two bottle meeting.'"

Clara smiles, "One evening, Vern and I were sitting in the lobby with a couple of guys from the band and I was kidding around, singing the *Hukilau Song*. Vern started singing it in Swedish. One of the guys said 'Hey, that sounds great. Why don't you do that for Harry?'

"Harry was always introducing a new number, or changing the format, so we'd have rehearsals now and then. Sometimes, we'd break after the show, and then come back to the Mural Room and rehearse until five o'clock in the morning. During one of those rehearsals, I started doing the *Hukilau Song* and, after I finished my solo, Vern did his solo in Swedish. Harry loved it. We rehearsed it some more. Harry had the whole bandstand and start the song by singing in chorus, then I would do my solo, and then Vern would do his solo. It became a very popular part of our routine and we'd often include it two or three times a week."

Vern remembered it this way. "We were broadcasting over NBC every night from 11:30 until 11:55, and we played the *Hukilau Song* during that segment. Unbeknownst to me, my father happened to be listening that night. I hadn't written him anything about singing the song. Next day he called me. 'Hey—was that really MY boy singing in Swedish from coast to coast? I told him it was. He was shocked, but pleased."

Yes—San Francisco wove a lot of memories during those war years—some happy—some sad.

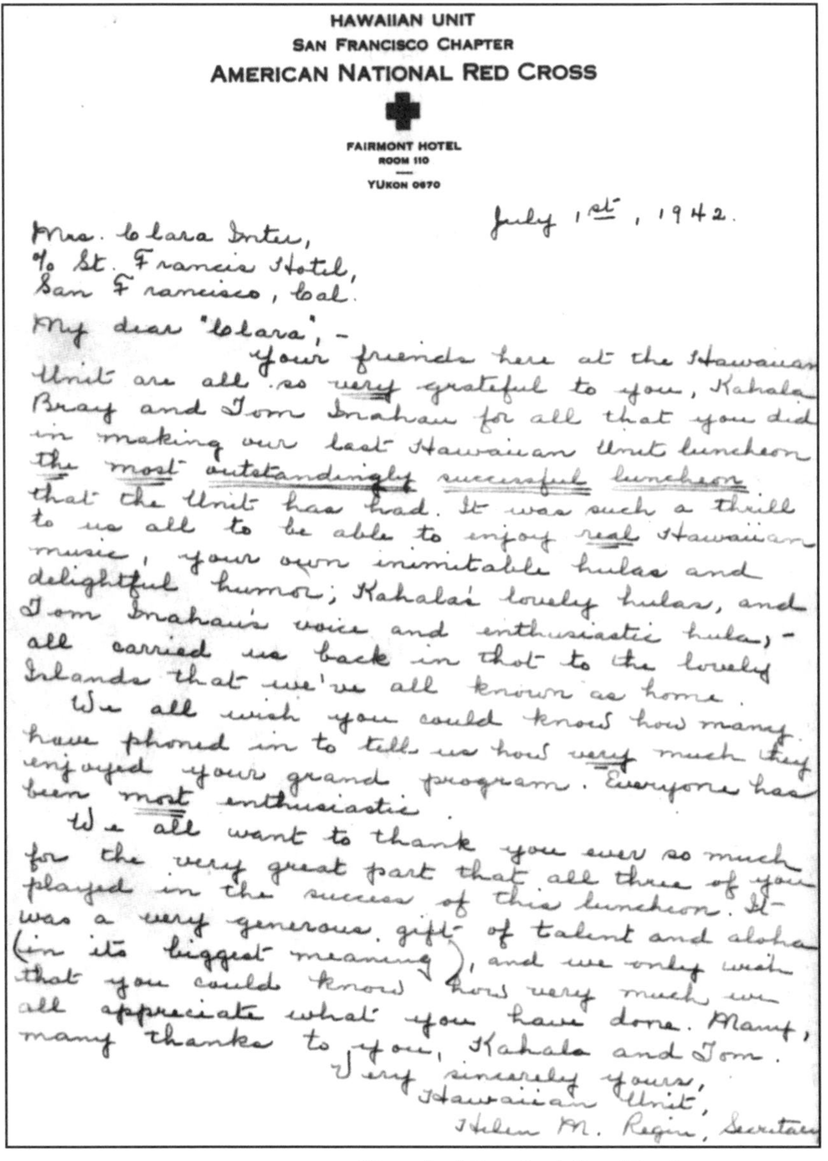

HAWAIIAN UNIT
SAN FRANCISCO CHAPTER
AMERICAN NATIONAL RED CROSS

FAIRMONT HOTEL
ROOM 110
YUKON 0670

July 1st, 1942.

Mrs. Clara Inter,
c/o St. Francis Hotel,
San Francisco, Cal.

My dear "Clara",-

Your friends here at the Hawaiian Unit are all so very grateful to you, Kahala Bray and Tom Inahau for all that you did in making our last Hawaiian Unit luncheon the most outstandingly successful luncheon that the Unit has had. It was such a thrill to us all to be able to enjoy real Hawaiian music, your own inimitable hulas and delightful humor; Kahala's lovely hulas, and Tom Inahau's voice and enthusiastic hula,- all carried us back in thot to the lovely Islands that we've all known as home.

We all wish you could know how many have phoned in to tell us how very much they enjoyed your grand program. Everyone has been most enthusiastic.

We all want to thank you ever so much for the very great part that all three of you played in the success of this luncheon. It was a very generous gift of talent and aloha (in its biggest meaning), and we only wish that you could know how very much we all appreciate what you have done. Many, many thanks to you, Kahala and Tom.

Very sincerely yours,
Hawaiian Unit,
Helen M. Regin, Secretary

I'd receive letter after letter of thanks. (Hannah Smith)

They loved it when Joe Keahiolalo and I did *Manuela Boy.* (Hawaiian Electric Company)

chapter eleven

Those In Between Years—Mainland and Honolulu

There were lots of exciting episodes in Clara's life not covered in specific chapters. Like the year 1941 before Clara went to the Mainland, she was invited to Hilo on the Big Island to help celebrate the Hawai'i Civic Club's second annual Holokū Ball.

"I arrived on Saturday morning and was stunned with the crowd that had gathered at the airport. The newspapers later reported there was a crowd of over 5,000 persons. First, I was serenaded by Eva Kahauolopua's troupe as I got off the plane and then greeted by a huge welcoming committee. They presented me with a Koa key to the city, then the Deputy Sheriff pinned a shiny gold Deputy Sheriff's badge on me."

There were official Holokū Balls at the Hilo Hotel and at the Armory, and Clara performed at both of them. Both were packed. There were lots of awards and lots of announcements. Mrs. William Yuen won the Lei Queen contest that year, followed by the traditional announcement of the six winners wearing the most beautiful holokū gowns. "It was a beautiful experience."

During 1945 and 1946, Clara was doing a lot of singles along the West Coast—just Clara, her 'ukulele, her faithful Kerry Blue terrier and her trusty 1941 Chevy coupe. Many times Clara played in Portland, Oregon, and she had quite a few friends there.

"My first visit was way back in 1936 when I went to a teachers' convention. In 1946 I had been booked at a small club in Portland where

I had played before, but the new owner had never seen me perform. When he came to rehearsal in the afternoon and saw me performing in my bare feet, big sloppy muʻumuʻu and battered hat, he called me aside and offered me some money in advance to go out and buy some clothes.

"That night we played to a packed audience as usual. The owner was standing at the entrance, pacing the floor and wringing his hands. Later, one of the stage hands told me his only comment was, 'How can a fat barefooted foreigner in a nightgown and a battered hat get an ovation like that?'"

In 1946, Clara went back to Hawaiʻi for a vacation and did a six-week show at the Royal Hawaiian Hotel. One day Clara received a call from Hal Lewis, a young gentleman in advertising, newly arrived in Hawaiʻi. He suggested she become a disc jockey. That Hal Lewis is now the famous J. Akuhead Pūpūle, master disc jockey of Radio Station K59. Here's the way it all happened according to Aku:

"A lot of people really don't know that Clara was the 'mother of Aku,' and I'll tell you how it happened. When I first came to Hawaiʻi in 1946, I was working for an advertising agency that obtained a new account called Western Dairy Products. We wanted a new idea for a radio show. The only Hawaiian entertainer's name I had ever heard was Hilo Hattie, so I got this bright idea that she should be a disc jockey. I called her, suggesting the idea. At first, she was shocked."

"Me—a disc jockey?"

"Then I explained I would write the lines and all she had to do was read them, and we would record. Then I'd put the whole show together with music, and every day she'd be a disc jockey for an hour on KPOA.

"She agreed and we planned to tape about 180 shows, but she got a call from Harry Owens to come back to the Mainland, and we only had 150 or 160 shows taped.

"Now the station was paying me to produce this show. I just walked in and told them we'd have to cancel the show because Clara was leaving and we didn't have all the shows taped. They asked me to finish the show. Then they asked me if I'd be willing to fill in on the morning show. The guy who was doing that show had to make an emergency trip to the mainland because his father was sick.

"To make a long story short—that guy never came back, and that's how I got to be Aku. That was over thirty years ago and I've been in radio or show business ever since.

"We did many shows together after that, but every time we got together we always had a minute to kid about Hilo Hattie, the disc jockey."

In 1947 Clara had a chance to come back to Hawai'i again for . This time she was asked to do a show for the Hawaiian Electric Company. Every year, HECO has a big party presenting awards to many of their faithful employees. That year was one of the biggest, with 131 faithful employees receiving awards. The party was held at the then famous Queen's Surf Restaurant. Many local celebrities performed there. It was a landmark. Their Barefoot Bar, with red-painted feet leading the way, was world famous.

The building was originally constructed in 1915 for a Chicago millionaire, C. W. Case Deering. It had quite a history between that time and its demolition in 1971. During the war years, it served as a rest and relaxation center for the Navy. Many important conferences were held there. President Roosevelt, General MacArthur, and Admiral Nimitz met there in 1944 to discuss strategy in the Pacific. After several ownerships, the Government finally bought the property and in 1946 leased it to Spencecliff Corporation with permission to use it as a restaurant. The restaurant was named The Queen's Surf.

In 1969, Mayor Frank Fasi decided that area of the beach should be made into open space for a park. The Queen's Surf would be demolished. There were violent protests and many fights in council meetings, but it was torn down in 1971.

But on this night, Monday, November 10, 1947, the Queen's Surf was very much alive with the Hawaiian Electric Company party. Bill Akamahou's five-piece band was playing music interspersed with awards. The hit of the evening was what HECO called, "Our Own Hilo Hattie. We can call her that because she's entertained us many times since that first time in 1938, when Clara came out dressed in a white holokū blazoned with the bright red figure of Reddy Kilowatt, which brought the house down. You never know what's going to happen when Hilo Hattie's around."

Clara supplemented her dancing with a special impromptu welcoming speech to her many HECO friends. The highlight of the evening, though, was when Joe Keahiolalo was persuaded to come up and do a hula with Clara. *Manuela Boy* as performed by Joe & Clara was certainly the hit of that night's festive affair.

Once again, Clara was able to return to Hawai'i in October of 1951. October 28 was Clara's fiftieth birthday, and sister Thelma thought it would be a wonderful time to have a huge lū'au. All preparations were going full speed ahead. Came the day of the party, it was pouring rain—not that fine "Hawaiian snow"—but coming down in buckets.

The Reverend Abraham Akaka has a beautiful saying for rainy days: "When the heavens cry, the earth flourishes." This is true, but somehow pouring rain is not conducive to an outdoor lū'au. So in true Hawaiian fashion, Thelma simply marched next door where Roy and Ruth Turner had a huge house, and announced, "You're having a lū'au tonight."

They had a sit-down indoor lū'au that evening with approximately fifty guests. Among those guests were Lois and Ernest Gray, who met Clara for the first time. Lois still remembers the party with amazement.

"All that food and entertainment! Clara's charismatic charm just beamed the minute you met her. I'll never forget it. When we raised a toast to her birthday, Clara got up and made a one-minute speech to everyone in the room, calling them by name, and saying something humorous to each of us. Since it was the first time she met me, I was overwhelmed. My husband said later it was the shortest fifty-minute speech he had ever heard.

"Later in the evening, Clara donned a kimono to do her famous Japanese number. They had an extra kimono that my husband put on. He started mimicking everything she did. That was really funny; everyone was hysterical.

"Later, when we bought a ranch and moved to Maui, we always enjoyed a visit from Clara and Carlyle. Clara used to call Ernest the biggest 'bullshipper' on the island."

Something different in lūʻau was always turning up. In 1955 Clara was performing in Los Angeles and doing the television show with Harry Owens. Hank Gogerty, owner of the Desert Aire Motel at Rancho Mirage, decided to put on a big lūʻau. His friend, Waltah Clarke, had just started a line of Hawaiian clothes that year, and Waltah told Hank about a wonderful hula dancer in Los Angeles that would know how to handle the whole affair Hawaiian style.

Hank called Kāhala Bray Yancy, and between Kāhala and her husband, Tom, they started making plans for a traditional lūʻau. The Yancys had a good friend in Honolulu, Frank Stober, who was with the transportation department of Pan Am. He is now a minister in Honolulu, but at that time he was working for Pan American. Through Frank's cooperation in Hawaiʻi and the Yancys' in Los Angeles, a whole tropical scene was moved in—ti leaves, ginger, plumeria, fresh lei for all the ladies. There was pineapple, coconuts, bananas, papaya—even poi.

Kāhala arranged for all the entertainment, too. Then Tom had a great idea. "How would you like to have Hilo Hattie at the lūʻau?"

"I'd love it," Frank replied. "But she's on the Harry Owens' television show that night."

"I think I might be able to arrange it," Tom said.

Tom had a good friend who not only owned the Whitman Airport, he also owned a plane. Just for being invited to the lūʻau he offered to fly down, pick up Hilo and bring her to the lūʻau.

Clara taxied to the airport immediately after the show, hopped in the plane and headed for Rancho Mirage. The plane had had a public address system installed and, as they approached the Desert Aire Motel, Hilo Hattie started singing the *Hilo Hattie Hop*. As the plane circled lower, all the people at the lūʻau looked up, wondering what was going on. The plane landed close to the swimming pool and Hilo Hattie walked out, continuing to sing her number. The people couldn't believe it. The television had been tuned to the Harry Owens' show and they had watched her on television thirty minutes before.

Needless to day, a wonderful time was had by all, including Hilo Hattie.

Roy and June Shipstad (Shipstads and Johnson Ice Follies) were very dear friends of Clara's for many years. In 1953, Roy thought it might be interesting to add a Hilo Hattie number to the show. Since they were playing in San Francisco at the time, a cable car theme seemed just right. That season, they added a new number with Clara being pulled to center ring in a cable car, and then doing her special number. June thought it was such fun. "Every time we did it, she received a standing ovation."

June also has fond memories of a 1955 surprise visit from Clara at Windsor, Canada. "I had broken my foot and was in a private room at the Hôtel-Dieu, a Catholic hospital. Our show was touring the northern states when the accident happened. I was lying in the hospital bed one night when I heard 'ukulele music coming down the hall. The door flew open—there was Clara in her bare feet, a mink coat down to her ankles, a silly pink straw hat on her head, playing the 'ukulele and singing. That was the last scene I would ever have dreamed of seeing. I just burst out in laughter. Clara was like that. She was always doing something to make you laugh. She even said, 'Move over' and crawled in bed,

June Shipstad broke her foot and I paid a visit. (June Shipstad)

sticking her leg up in the air to mimic me. She stayed till about midnight and then slipped quietly out the back door.

"After that, Clara came every night. She'd entertain in every room as she came down the hall, ending up in my room. Each night she'd stay till about midnight. Windsor was my hometown and Clara stayed with my folks.

"I had lots of relatives in Windsor, so I'd have lots of company each night. My nurses' aide was called Mickey Finn, of all things. She would arrange the chairs in a semicircle around the bed, and Clara would perform. It was just like a theater. Every night Clara would perform, dancing, singing, telling jokes. When I was about ready to leave, Mother Superior came to say goodbye. She said, 'I don't know whether I'm going to be happy or sad to see you go. I've never lost so much sleep since I've been here, but I've never had so much fun either.'

"Clara was known to be a good cook, so one day my folks invited her to prepare dinner. She just took everything in the refrigerator and put it in one big pot. There was salmon and steak and vegetables and everything imaginable. Mother said they had a terrible time eating it. It must have been the worst meal Clara ever cooked.

"Clara and I used to do a lot of cooking together," June recalls. "Rather, I should say, Clara cooked and I helped. Sometimes she called me 'chop-chop June,' because I'd chop or mince all those ingredients for her Oriental dishes for hours, and she'd cook them in minutes. She always told me I was the worst rice cooker in the world. Time after time she'd give me another chance to make good rice, and time after time I'd make a mess of it. One day a rice cooker arrived in the mail with an affectionate note, 'Bet you can't ruin the rice using this.'"

Here we are cutting the wedding cake. (Carlyle Nelson)

chapter twelve

1949 Brought the Wonderful Marriage to Carlyle Nelson

Carlyle Nelson first came to Hawai'i to play at the Royal Hawaiian Hotel with Chick Floyd's band in June of 1947.

Born in North Dakota, the Nelson family moved to Visalia when Carlyle was nine years old. His mother, an accomplished musician, decided the violin would be a good instrument for Carlyle to play, and so he started taking lessons at an early age. By the time he was in high school, Carlyle was playing in the school orchestra and for a few dances on the side. After graduating from high school, he attended the New England Conservatory of Music in Boston for two years—then returned to Visalia to teach violin.

During the war, Carlyle was in the Army Air Corps and stationed at Lemoore Field, where he played in the band. There were many concerts, too. His solo performances often brought words of praise in newspapers, like the time he performed for the Bakersfield Community Symphony at the Standard School Auditorium. By this time he had added saxophone and clarinet to his repertoire.

After he married Clara he branched out into the steel guitar, at which he is now considered an expert. "I had to learn the steel guitar in self defense," Carlyle said. "It was so hard to get steel guitar players. I know why now. It's a very difficult instrument."

As we said, Carlyle was playing with the Chick Floyd band and Clara was still playing at the St. Francis Hotel in San Francisco with Harry Owens. In October she returned to Hawai'i for some engagements during Aloha Week and ended up accepting a contract with Alvin Isaacs and his Royal Hawaiian Serenaders, who were also performing at the Royal Hawaiian. Chick's band was playing on the outside terrace and the Serenaders would play alternately from the Monarch Room inside. Clara would usually perform in the doorway where she was visible to the entire audience.

Carlyle remembers those first few months. "We had a temporary, portable canvas bandstand and I used to sit on it and watch Clara perform. I never realized I was conspicuous, but when we got to know each other better, she often referred to me as 'the guy who sat on the bandstand.' One night I watched her perform and could tell she was feeling terrible. As soon as her number was over, she went over to the side and sat down, holding her stomach. She was in great pain. They called an ambulance and Clara was operated on that night."

While she recovered, Clara went to Los Angeles and stayed with some very wonderful friends, Percy and Hannah Smith.

In November 1948, Chick's band moved on to Dallas, Texas, where they played at the Baker Hotel.

"Unknown to us," Carlyle recalls, "Clara was the headliner in the show. I didn't know Clara very well then. It wasn't until we went on the road with Chick that I really got to know her. Our assignment at the Baker Hotel was for five weeks and it was one of those long hour jobs. We played six noons and seven nights a week, three shows a day, except Sunday which was only two shows.

"One Sunday afternoon I asked Clara if she'd go to the theater with me. *Carousel* was playing in Dallas that season and it was receiving rave reviews. Clara said she'd love to see it. That was the beginning of our close relationship."

The group was very close. With those long hours, there wasn't much time left for outside entertainment. The Floyds were living at the Baker Hotel and, oftentimes, they would invite the whole band up to their room for a party after the show. Allene Floyd remembers a special Christmas party in their suite when Clara took her aside, saying, "I think Carlyle's pretty cute. I think I'll set my cap for him."

"I was surprised," says Allene, "Carlyle certainly is a prince of a man, but he is so shy and retiring, and Clara is just the opposite."

From there the show moved to Reno. Carlyle shared an apartment with Hal Johnson, the saxophonist. "I always carried a pressure cooker, hot plate, and an omelet pan. We were playing at the Golden Hotel and Clara was living there. I'd cook lots of times in those days, and invite Clara up to the apartment for meals. I did the same thing at our next stop in Sacramento. We were playing at the El Rancho and Clara was staying there. Hal and I got another apartment, and again I'd cook and invite Clara to join us. Once in a while Clara would do the cooking, and I soon realized she was a better cook than I."

It was in Sacramento that Carlyle proposed to Clara. The Floyds were having another party in their hotel room. "Yeah," Chick recalls. "It was sorta funny. Carlyle actually proposed to her in the closet of our hotel room, but they didn't tell us then."

"That's right," Carlyle agrees, "I proposed to her right there in the closet of their hotel suite—but it was a big closet! I was surprised when she said yes. We thought we'd keep it a secret for awhile. We wanted to finish the job in Sacramento, then go back to Los Angeles."

They decided to get married in Las Vegas and asked their good friends, Max and Babe Reid, if they'd go along. "They agreed, so we all jumped in my Oldsmobile and drove to Las Vegas. We were married on April 5, 1949, in a small chapel with just a few friends present."

The picture at the beginning of this chapter, showing Carlyle and Clara cutting their wedding cake, was taken at the dinner that followed the ceremony. "I don't even remember the name of the hotel," says Carlyle, "but I know it was one of those fancy ones on the strip and a gift from our friends, the Ahlswedes, who live in Las Vegas."

Clara returned to Los Angeles to join Harry Owens and Carlyle went to Lake Tahoe to join Chick Floyd's band. Clara spent the summer at the St. Francis Hotel in San Francisco. "Lake Tahoe and San Francisco weren't so far apart, so often on weekends I'd go down to San Francisco, and other times Clara would come up and enjoy the beautiful fresh air at Lake Tahoe.

"Our contracts ended about the same time, so we both returned to Los Angeles, and I joined Harry Owens' band. At first we stayed with our friends, the Reids, then we moved to a tiny house on Cahuenga Park Trail, which Clara bought during the war.

"My playing with Harry Owens didn't work out too well. Perhaps we were both too dependent upon Clara. I thought I would like to do some outside bookings. At first it was with Harry's blessing, but he changed his mind. I felt it best to drop out of Harry's orchestra, and found a very interesting job doing the music for an ice show called Frosty Follies. It was a weekly show in Pasadena. It was harder work than with Harry, but it was pleasant work and I enjoyed it a lot. Harry and I got along much better then. It kept us from being too close to each other constantly."

Clara continued with Harry. Occasionally, Carlyle would have a single show and Clara would perform with him. They followed pretty much the same routine until the summer of 1951.

In June of 1951, Harry Owens decided to take a vacation in Hawai'i and recommended to the St. Francis Hotel that Frank Sabatella take over as leader of the Royal Hawaiians, with Hilo Hattie as mistress of ceremonies and star of the show. Frank was a marvelous musician and did an excellent job leading the band. Carlyle rejoined the group. They did take time out that year to return to Hawai'i when Clara's mother died.

During 1952 and 1953 they were both working at the Hotel Roosevelt. Clara was the headliner in the Islander Room, and Carlyle was leading the band in the CineGrill. "By that time we had purchased a large home on Primera Street in Hollywood. It was a large Spanish house—over 3,000 square feet—and spread over three levels on the side of a hill. We did a lot of remodeling and expanding that old house. It was a happy house. I'll never forget the time Clara did a part on The Tennessee Ernie Ford Show and was paid with a huge Amana double freezer. This was where we were living at the time and they sent the driver out alone to deliver this new freezer. We had to enlist all the help in the neighborhood to get that big thing up the steps.

"When the CineGrill job ended, the owners wanted me to take my orchestra to the El Rancho in Sacramento, but Clara's show was still under contract and I didn't want to be that far away. So I found a job working for a taxi dancehall downtown—right in the skid row area. Actually, it didn't sound like much, but it was really a good job. It paid very well and I didn't have to be there all the time, so I could continue my job with the Frosty Follies. That made a long day though. At the dancehall we played until two in the morning. The next day the ice show started rehearsing at nine, broke for lunch at twelve, rehearsed again until six, broke for dinner and did the show at eight. Then I dashed over to the dancehall to play again until two A.M.

"Until 1960 it was pretty much the same routine—traveling on the road six months of the year, casuals in the Los Angeles and San Francisco areas, the television broadcasts with Harry Owens until he did his last one in July of 1958, and an occasional trip to Hawai'i to ease Clara's nostalgia."

But let's continue with Clara's story.

Gail and I enjoy some old-fashioned gabfests. (Gail Nelson)

chapter thirteen

Gail Nelson Enters the Picture and Makes a Lasting Impression

Clara first met Carlyle's daughter, Gail, in 1949 before they were married. Carlyle wanted Clara to meet his family in Visalia, so after their show in Sacramento, they went to Visalia, then on to Bakersfield to meet his daughter. Gail was twelve at the time, a very lively, vivacious youngster with sparkling brown eyes. "We didn't talk much at the first meeting," said Clara, "but she made a very sweet and indelible impression on me. The summer of 1950 we asked Gail to spend her vacation with us in San Francisco.

"All of a sudden at age forty-eight, it can be a little startling to become a mother. My relationship with Gail became a blend of friend-buddy and, yes, sometimes mother, too.

"Carlyle and I were so excited about the prospect of having her with us for the first time, we rented a house. Normally, we lived at the St. Francis Hotel where we were playing, but thought having a house might be more welcoming to Gail. We really didn't need to do that. Gail found the hotel absolutely fascinating. Naturally, Carlyle and I spent much time at the hotel—playing six nights a week, sometimes in the afternoons. Always, the highlight of the week was the Saturday afternoon tea dance. Then, there were rehearsals, too. We still kept a room at the hotel so Gail could relax anytime she wanted to. Usually, she preferred being with us, flitting throughout the hotel. All of the employees loved her and really gave her the run of the hotel. Sometimes, she would have a table in the audience with a friend while we were performing or she would just sit offstage. Her favorite avocation for that summer was riding the cable cars. I think she knew every cable car driver in San Francisco. We often took the cable car to our home, and Gail would call the driver by name."

When Clara asked Gail's reflections on the highlight of that summer, Gail's eyes lit up—"The alligator shoes."

"Alligator shoes?" Clara asked.

"Yes—the alligator high-heeled shoes. That was my very first pair of high-heeled shoes and I felt so grown up at age thirteen. Remember? You bought me my first pair of nylon hose, too."

"Suddenly, it all came back in a flash. Indeed, I did remember the high-heeled shoes and the nylon stockings. In those days, they all had seams and what a time we had getting them straight."

Gail laughs. "Yes, those seams were something. You were so patient showing me how to put them on carefully so they wouldn't get snagged, and 'always, always, check your seams,' you admonished."

"Most summers after that Gail was able to spend some time with us. Even when we were traveling on the road, Gail would visit us for a week or two."

During Gail's high school days in Bakersfield, she met and dated, very frequently, Don Johnston. In 1954, Gail entered UCLA in Los Angeles. Although she was living in a dormitory on campus, she loved going over to Daddy and Clara's big house in North Hollywood. Oftentimes, she would bring seven or eight of her girlfriends to spend the weekend, and they were always welcome. "They were always working, but would find the time to do something special with the gang I would bring," Gail remembers.

Gail remembers the year of 1954 as another highlight of her life. "I was just seventeen and my greatest desire was to have my own car. Dad was afraid of spoiling me, so he let me have his old 1937 DeSoto. Clara kept hinting for a new car for me, but Dad would say, 'No—she can have this one.' What a joy it was. I was the only girl in the dormitory that had her own car. I remember the gas gauge didn't work, so anytime we would want to drive someplace, I'd ask everybody for a quarter, and we'd drive to the nearest gas station and buy as much gas as we had quarters. I got a lot of mileage with that car. In fact, I kept it until 1955 when I was married."

Carlyle remembers the 1937 DeSoto with much affection. "Yes, she didn't need it after she was married, so I took it back and drove it another five years."

Gail recalls, "I was reminded of that incident much later when my own son wanted his first car. Clara and Daddy happened to be with us the first time my son, Dennis, mentioned it. Clara looked at Daddy and said, 'Well Grandpa?' Daddy cleared his throat saying, 'Well, I think we better let Dennis' father take charge of this matter,' and promptly marched out of the room. Don and I talked it over that evening and both agreed that Daddy's philosophy was right. Dennis did not need a new car for his first one."

Gail Nelson and Don Johnston were married at St. Paul's Episcopal Church in Bakersfield, California, on August 7, 1955. "What a beautiful Hawaiian decor we had," Gail remembers. "Clara sent to Hawai'i for lots and lots of flowers. There were orchid trees covered with vandas, ti leaves all around the altar, and plumeria blossoms strung down the aisle. It was so beautiful and smelled fragrant, too."

Two years later, a grandson, Dennis, was born on February 14, 1957, and on December 16, 1958, a granddaughter, Tari Lynn. For that occasion, Carlyle and Clara went to Bakersfield and stayed two weeks.

Gail remembers many wonderful vacations with Daddy and Clara—mostly, they included the children. "In 1962, when Daddy and Clara were playing at the Orange County Fair, our whole family went to Newport Beach for the weekend. Clara took us to Disneyland. It was my children's first visit and they were really excited. Sometimes, we'd visit them in Hawai'i, too.

"My first boat trip was with Dad and Clara in 1969. We took the *Italia* cruise from San Francisco to Alaska. Dennis and Tari Lynn were with us and what those two children didn't learn at the hands of Grandma Clara hadn't been invented yet. They gambled on the horse races; they played ping pong and hide and go seek; they went to see the Captain's quarters.

"Daddy and Clara were supposed to be on vacation but it was soon learned that Mrs. Clara Nelson was the famous Hilo Hattie. Several times she was asked if she was going to entertain, so finally one night, she agreed to put on a little show in one of the conference rooms.

"The main entertainment with the ship's orchestra was going on in the main salon. Our little conference room was getting fuller and fuller. It seemed everybody aboard ship was trying to get into the room or jamming the hallways. Finally, they moved Clara and Dad over to the main salon and the ship's orchestra played for them. The orchestra was Italian and spoke very little English. The piano player could speak a little French, so Dad could converse a little with him. Daddy let the piano player work from his violin music."

Carlyle remembers the incident vividly. "Yes, I remember we did *Ke Kali Nei Au* and it wasn't in our range and it was terrible."

Gail interrupts, "No, it wasn't terrible, Daddy. The passengers loved it. They laughed and laughed."

Carlyle adds, "I'll never forget the way that guy beat the hell out of the piano. The *Cockeyed Mayor* never sounded like that before."

In reflecting over the past years, Gail is quick to admit that she too succumbed to Clara's charm. To quote Gail:

"I don't know of a more beautiful lady here on this earth. Her gifts of happiness through the years, to so many, many people in the audience and individually, are more than one can express. People have always felt close to her whether she is entertaining on stage or sitting in a restaurant. She would have words of kindness for the parking attendant as much as for the Captain of a ship. She always felt it was HER pleasure to be able to entertain for so many people.

"I think one of her proudest accomplishments was being able to entertain our servicemen aboard every battleship that served in the Pacific during World War II.

"Her attitude, with others, has always been that there is something special about everyone. She so freely expresses her love to others.

"Clara and my father have the most beautiful love affair one will ever experience. Their total devotion to each other for these past thirty years is a most beautiful relationship.

"She has a God-given gift of pure graciousness."

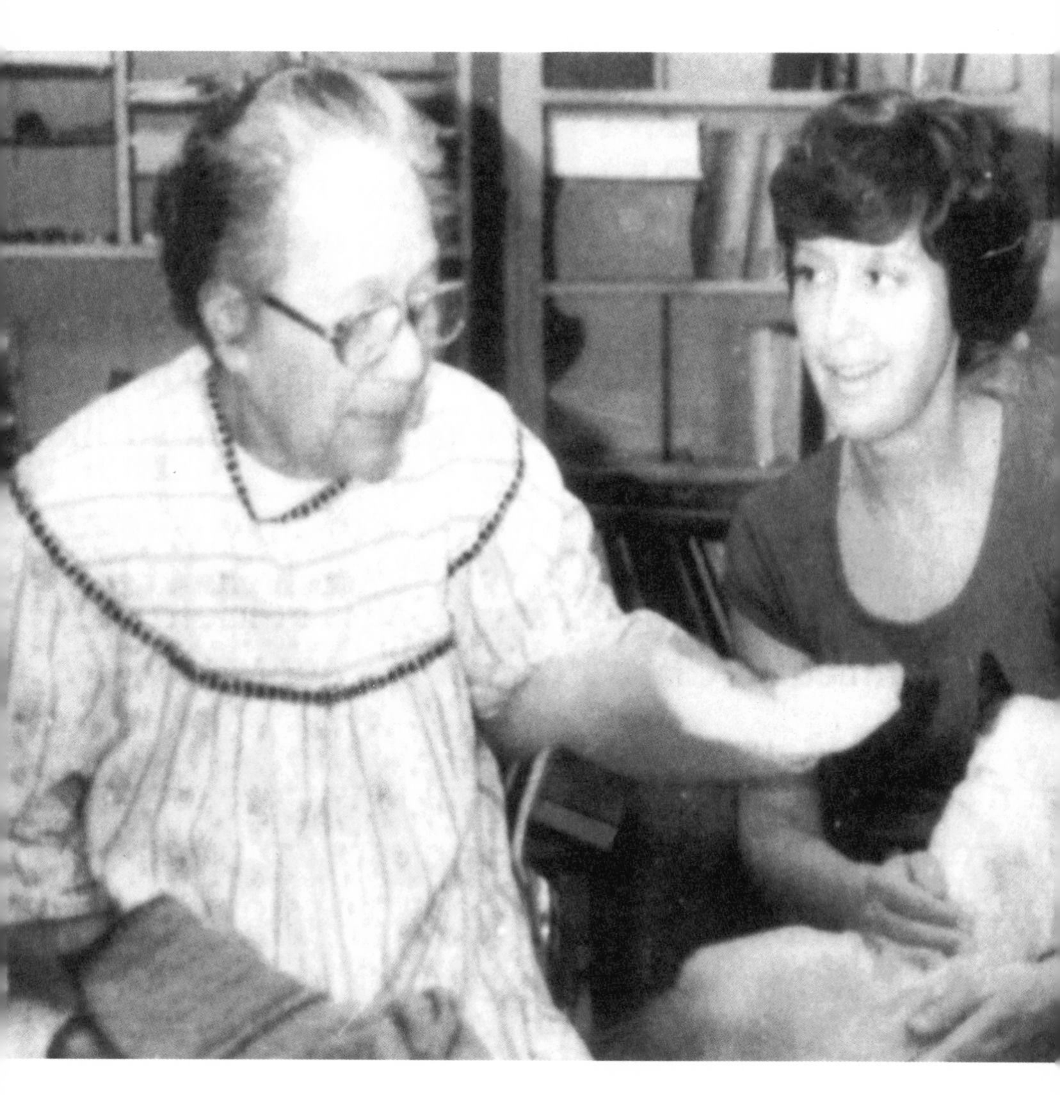

Gail comes to visit me after the stroke. (Gail Nelson)

Holiday Inn gives us a grand welcome. (Carlyle Nelson)

chapter fourteen

What It's Like Working Six Months on the Road

It's hard! Just let me tell you it's hard! But it's fun too. You get to meet so many people and they're all laughing and having fun. Even in 1942 when I worked with Harry Owens at the St. Francis, we would travel several months out of the year. Later, when I had my own show and traveled with my husband's band, we had a regular routine of six months on the road and several months at a regular engagement.

Travel with me, if you will for a typical month—like June of 1962. Remember, I was no spring chicken, but I was feeling swell. We traveled in two Cadillacs, each with a trailer.

Friday, June 1—San Antonio—Abilene. 250 miles. We arrived at 2 P.M. and checked into the Holiday Inn. We all had dinner at the NCO Club that evening and played from 9 P.M. to 1 A.M. at Dyess AFB.

Saturday, June 2—Abilene—Lubbock. 150 miles. Made several long distance calls and wrote some letters. Seven of us went out to dinner. Played at Reese AFB that night.

Sunday, June 3—Lubbock—Amarillo. 120 miles. Arrived at 5 P.M. and stayed at the Holiday Inn. What a surprise! As we approached the motel, in great big letters on their marquee it read WELCOME HILO HATTIE AND HAWAIIANS. I thought that was so nice of them. We played at the NCO Club at Amarillo AFB 9:30 P.M. to 12:30 A.M. Had a snack at the Plainsman and left for Alamogordo at 1:45 A.M.

Monday, June 4—Amarillo-Alamogordo. 321 miles. Had breakfast at Sunset, New Mexico. Dinner at Desert Aire. Very good. Show at Holloman AFB at 9:30 P.M. Home at 11:30 P.M. Wrote some letters.

Tuesday, June 5—Alamogordo—El Paso. 84 miles. We had breakfast next door at the Plainsman at 8 A.M., gassed up and arrived in El Paso at 11 A.M. Had the day off, so got a lot of miscellaneous things accomplished. Played nine holes of golf. Washed clothes. Did some miscellaneous shopping. We stayed at the Caballero Motel. Had a lovely dinner at Moon Gate. $30. Good.

Wednesday, June 6th—Had breakfast at 6:15. Took a nap. Did some grocery shopping and cooked dinner. The Tahitian skirts arrived today. It was Violet's birthday so we had to celebrate a little. That evening we drove out to Fort Bliss and did a show at the NCO Club.

Thursday, June 7—Still in El Paso. We play at the Officer's Club tonight. Had a big lunch and just ate a little dessert before going to work. Made several long distance calls and wrote some letters. Brought my diary up to date.

Friday, June 8th—Played at the NCO Club at White Sands. It was 50 miles over desert road so we left at 5:30 P.M. as we were not sure of the way. Played 9 P.M. to 1 A.M. Had breakfast after the show and talked till 2:45 A.M.

Saturday, June 9—Played the Officer's Club at Biggs AFB.

Sunday, June 10—El Paso—Alamogordo. 84 miles. Did a brief show 2 P.M. to 2:30 P.M. at the Whispering Sands Community Center. Very nice stage. Played the Officer's Club at the AFB 7 P.M. to 11 P.M. I had a chance to rest upstairs in the music room from 4 P.M. till 5:30 P.M. Had a nice weiner roast. We hadn't checked out of the motel, so had to drive back, arriving in El Paso at 2 A.M. Read mail that had accumulated.

Monday, June 11—Day off. Wonderful. We got a big box of food from my sister, Thelma. Oh, how I bless that wonderful sister of mine. We get so homesick for Hawaiian food and Thelma often sends us a box. Always there's poi, usually some dried fish, and then some canned things. When we get a can of salmon, I cut it up with green onions, tomatoes, and Hawaiian salt, trying to get it something like our lomi lomi salmon, Took the Juarez tour at 3 P.M. It was interesting. Did some shopping while there. Had dinner at Moon Gate. $40. Not so good. Next time I'll order. I went to bed early. Girls went to the movies.

Tuesday, June 12—6 A.M. breakfast. Played golf 7 A.M. to 11 A.M. Lots of mail today. Received Long Beach contract, Special Service contract was goofed up. Had letters from Mom and Gail. Played at No. 1 Service Club at 6:30 P.M. and No. 2 Service Club at 8:30 P.M. Violet fixed poi and we had a nice meal in our rooms—mostly from the box Thelma had sent. Sheila rehearsed and I had a nice session with the girls.

Wednesday, June 13—Breakfast and talked with Bill and Sheila. Car needs some work. Had to make several phone calls and write letters. Have an 8 P.M. show at the El Paso Service Center, just 30 miles away.

Thursday, June 14—El Paso—Tuscon. 325 miles. 6 A.M. breakfast. Left at 7:00 in the morning, arriving in Tucson at 2 P.M. Stayed at the Sage and Sand Motel. We had the night off, so checked out the Randolph Golf Course for tomorrow. Looks nice. I fixed a big stew dinner for all.

Friday, June 15—Boys golfed at Randolph. Violet and I shopped. Both boys and girls had to rehearse. I cooked pork chops that night. We had two shows that night at Davis Monthan AFB. One at the Officer's Club and another at the NCO Club. We had to dress in the office and it became rather confusing.

Saturday, June 16—Boys golfed again. I slept till 9 A.M. Did the payroll. Wrote some letters. Had the car washed. Wrote to San Diego for accommodations for all of us from July 1 through July 4. Another show at Davis Monthan AFB 9 P.M. to 1 A.M. Officer's Club.

Sunday, June 17—Another show at Davis Monthan, this time at the NCO Club. Stage not so good. Received several letters and wrote quite a few. Did some grocery shopping. Bought chicken, pork, vegetables, melon. Eddie and I cooked dinner. Boys and Violet played golf.

Monday, June 18—Day off. Boys and Violet played golf again. I did some repairs, wrote letters and worked on my diary.

Tuesday, June 19—Another day off. We all played golf today. Had a nice chop suey dinner. Good. Kids did laundry.

Wednesday, June 20—And another day off. We all golfed again. I did some shopping, including a shirt for Thelma. Ate leftovers and weiners. Cleaned the kitchen and packed for an early departure tomorrow.

Thursday, June 21—Tucson—Yuma. 243 miles. We left at 5:45 A.M. and arrived in Yuma at 11:30. Stayed at the Silver Spur Motel. Had lunch at Woo's. $13. Chamber of Commerce had a party for us. We felt quite honored. Had dinner at Woo's too. Good. We put on a show at the Yuma Golf and Country Club 8 P.M. to 12 A.M.

Friday, June 22—Yuma—Phoenix. 181 miles. Had breakfast at Woo's at 6:15 A.M. that morning then we took off for Phoenix over Route 80. Checked in at the Cabana Lodge near the State Capitol building. Gave Eddie money to do some grocery shopping. I ate dinner by myself at Palowine Inn. We played at Luke Field Officer's Club that night. There were a lot of people who knew someone in Hawai'i, including people some of us knew. It was a very friendly get together.

Saturday, June 23—Breakfast at 8 A.M. Wrote several letters. Loafed all day. Didn't have much pep. We play at the Phoenix Country Club from 9 P.M. until 1 A.M. Show at 10 P.M. Norman Storey, manager, was very nice.

Sunday, June 24—Slept till 10 A.M. Loafed, washed and snacked. We play outdoors tonight at Luke Field. This time at the NCO Club.

Monday, June 25—Phoenix—29 Palms. 345 miles. Got up to pack at 5 A.M. Left at 6 A.M. Went through Joshua Tree National Park. Nice. Stayed at the Aloha Motel, checking in at 2 P.M. No work tonight. Eddie went shopping and did the cooking. We had a good dinner with lots of talking. Vi and the girls went to the movies. There was lots of mail and some contracts. I went to bed at 11 P.M.

Tuesday, June 26—Awake at 6:30 A.M. Washed clothes and loafed. Still not peppy. Went marketing again. This time for cold cuts, etc. It's hot. Tonight we play at the Marine Officer's Club 8:30 P.M. to 12:30 A.M. Show at 9:15 P.M.

Wednesday, June 27—29 Palms—San Francisco. 510 miles. Breakfast in Bakersfield. We had the night off. I decided to see some of San Francisco.

Thursday, June 28—Breakfast at Mannings. Had talk with the girls. They wanted me to repair some of their costumes. For some reason, the whole troupe treats me as 'Mother.' I love doing things for them. Did some shopping and phoning. Made reservations for Pismo Beach tomorrow. Worked at the marine Memorial 8:30 P.M. to 12:30 A.M.

Friday, June 29—San Francisco—Pismo Beach. 250 miles. Arrived at 1 P.M. and checked in the San Luis Obispo Motel, off the highway. We played at the Rose Garden Ballroom that night.

Saturday, June 30—Pismo Beach—Merced. 200 miles. Stayed at the Hotel Merced. Had a good Chinese dinner. $20. Played that night at Castle Air Force Base 9 P.M. to 1 A.M. Had a snack at the coffee shop after the show. Lousy. Left after that for Pacific Beach. Tomorrow night we play in San Diego.

And so the trip went. For those of you who have traveled extensively, you know the many details not covered: making reservations in advance, packing and unpacking, having clothes cleaned. But it was all balanced by those smiling, laughing faces from the audience. Several times people would come up from the audience saying they saw us in San Francisco or Los Angeles, and it would be like old times. Sometimes, when they knew we were going to another air base, they'd even send a message along for some buddy that had been reassigned.

It was a busy life. There were many laughs along the way, and sometimes a few tears and hurt feelings. Even though it was 1959, there was much racial hatred in the South. Being pure Hawaiian, my skin is not exactly white. After the show one night in Montgomery, Alabama, Carlyle and I decided to have a snack in a cafeteria on the way back to the motel. They did serve us, but when we paid the check the cashier wanted to know where we were from. We told them, and showed our business card and walked out the door. Outside waiting for us, was the owner of the restaurant, and a policeman with his hands on guns at his hips. I looked up at him—he seemed to be about twice my height. He didn't say a word, but the manager told us not to ever come back there.

1959 was the year Hawai'i became a state and we were still playing in Montgomery. There were two television stations in town and we called both of them, offering to do a free show as a special feature celebrating the event. Their reply was, "No thanks."

And that's what it's like, traveling six months on the road. At one time or another we've covered every state in the Union. Some in Canada, too.

We often toured together. First row (left to right): Melanie, Lokelani, and Lei Aloha. Second row (left to right): Clara, the late Pineapple Pete, Carlyle, Danny Santos, and Chief Satini. (Carlyle Nelson)

I enjoyed showing people how to make lei. (Hannah Smith)

chapter fifteen

Flowers and Ti Leaves Seemed to Bring Hawai'i Closer

"The haoles always enjoyed a demonstration on making lei. While we were at the St. Francis Hotel in San Francisco during the war, I often spent hours in the lobby making lei. We had a little corner of Hawaiiana, including a grass shack where they sold Victory Bonds. We had enough fresh flowers to demonstrate, but not enough to make lei for the show.

"One night Pat Patterson, president of United Airlines, caught the show in the Mural Room and I was wearing a paper lei. After the show he called me over to the table. 'Hey, Clara, what do you mean, wearing paper lei? You, a real Hawaiian.'

"'Auwe, Pat,' I answered, 'We can't get fresh Hawaiian flowers over here to make our lei.'

"'Just you leave that to me,' he said. 'Let me know your itinerary in advance and if there's a United plane landing in that town, you will have a fresh lei.'

"Buster McGuire of Honolulu would get them on the plane and somehow they'd always get to our hotel. And that's the way it was from then on. Pat was from Hawai'i and loved our traditions as much as we did. Pat Patterson certainly was a great friend to all of us.

"Ti leaves are a very important part of Hawaiian life. It made us so happy when the girls could wear the real ones for their hula skirts. Harry Owens insisted on fresh ti leaves when it was possible. In fact, it was one of his biggest headaches, particularly while we were traveling.

Big bundles of ti leaves arrived in gunny sacks, sometimes by ship, sometimes by plane.

"The photographs on the opposite page show how the girls started making the skirts. Back in those days they shredded them with a hairpin. Every hula dancer always knew how to make her ti leaf skirt. They were so much more graceful then. Through the years the shreds gradually kept getting wider and wider. It wasn't so much the time consuming work involved as the fact that the ti leaves kept longer if they weren't shredded. Lots of times when a shipment would arrive, we'd only shred half of them and keep the others whole for the following week. Nowadays they use the whole leaf, but I don't think it's nearly as graceful.

"The length of the skirt was very important. The girls never showed their knees in those days. Wouldn't show the belly buttons either. Even their dance was different. The movements were soft and gentle with a side-to-side swish like the movements of the waves, in comparison to the twirls they do nowadays where they show the panties.

"The bellboys and management of the hotels were all wonderful too. After the show, the girls would wash off the skirts, wrap them in newspaper and then in a towel, and the bellboys would put them in the icebox. The girls always tried to remember to take the skirts out of the icebox an hour or two before the show so they'd get back to room temperature. Once they were out doing some sightseeing and returned about fifteen minutes before show time. They grabbed the ti leaf skirts from the icebox, dashed to the dressing room, and did a lot of shivering before they got on the stage.

"There were many times in Los Angeles when we were able to make fresh lei from local flowers. My friend, Babe Reid, had two huge plumeria trees in her backyard. She'd always tell us to help ourselves. It was nice making those lei of plumeria. Reminded us of home. For some reason they do not grow plumeria trees abundantly on the Mainland, but Babe's trees offered us flowers for dozens of lei. When June and Roy Shipstad would stay with me during the six weeks the Shipstads and Johnson Ice Follies were playing in Los Angeles, I would often entice June into making the lei. She was good at it.

The ti leaves would arrive in gunny sacks.
(Kāhala Bray Yancy)

Kāhala and Leilani start stripping the leaves with a hairpin. (Kāhala Bray Yancy)

Carefully check the length—never show the knees!
(Kāhala Bray Yancy)

Leaves are assembled, tied just to fit your waist.
(Kāhala Bray Yancy)

"June told me I repaid her a million-fold by sending fresh flower lei to their Hawaiian act. In 1964, Roy Shipstad had created a new routine for the show designed around Hawaiian music and Hawaiian dancing. It was a beautiful number. Richard Dwyer and six skaters did the number, so when I heard about it I arranged to have six fresh double pink carnation lei flown in every day. At the end of the number, the girls would always take off the lei and give them to a gentleman in the audience, along with the traditional lei kiss.

"There was a period in 1940 when cellophane skirts were the thing. I believe it was Augie Auld who first brought them back to Hawai'i from Hollywood. Different yes—but, they'll never take the place of real ti leaves for me."

"I do love the flowers of Hawai'i, but flowers are beautiful everywhere. I always enjoyed the flowers when we were traveling. One spring we were playing a country club in Texas and I was overwhelmed by the abundance of flowers.

"We have lots of flowers in Hawai'i, but I've never seen anything like this," I said to the manager.

"Neither have I," he replied. "These are the most flowers I have ever seen in Texas. Even the weeds are full of blossoms. Come back in a couple of months and all you'll see is sagebrush and dust!"

"Sometimes we'd drive through the San Joaquin valley in the spring. What a glorious vista of orchards stretching for miles. Depending on the month it varied from the early almonds, to the peaches, cherries, apricots, and plums. Then as you went further south—around Lompoc, more profusion of flowers, but this time from commercial growers. Delphinium, ranunculas, daisies, sweet peas, pansies, marigolds—all planted neatly in rows and reflecting every color of the rainbow. It was fantastically beautiful. I'll never forget our visit to the Buchard Gardens in Victoria and the azalea trails in Georgia.

"Back in Ka'a'awa we have our own botanical garden. We have a Jackson and Perkins catalog from Oregon and are on their mailing list. I'm sure we get three or four flyers a month, and very often 'bite.' One year I surprised Carlyle with eight dwarf fruit trees."

"Surprise me indeed she did," Carlyle recalls. "So did the ground when I tried to dig. The trees required big holes, and there were so many rocks in the ground it took me days. They aren't doing too well, I might add. But we did get two pears, about an inch long, one year."

Clara with the Hawaiian Village Serenaders. (Carlyle Nelson)

chapter sixteen

1960—Opens Show at Tapa Room, Hawaiian Village

In 1955 the Hawaiian Village opened the Tapa Room with the singing sensation of that era, Alfred Apaka. Al was the most popular singer that year; his records sold millions. Unfortunately, his career was ended tragically by an early death in 1960. The Village tried performer after performer to take his place. First Aku, then Lucky Luck, Jimmy Kina, Jimmy Bulgo and Jimmy Moikeha, and that is when Hilo Hattie came on the scene.

"We had been on the road since April and our contract ended in November, which was just perfect. It was heaven to come back to Hawai'i. I remember well opening the show at the Tapa Room on November 26, 1960.

"In January of 1961, we recorded live from stage an album called *Hilo Hattie at the Hawaiian Village*. We included most of my most popular songs: *Hawaiian War Chant, Becky, Shinano Yoru, Cockeyed Mayor, When Hilo Hattie Does the Hilo Hop, Princess Pūpūle* and several others. Benny Kalama and his Hawaiian Village Serenaders played the background music. They had been playing at the Village for five years and continued all the time I was playing in the Tapa Room. That great bunch of guys included Pappy Bowman, David Kupele, Mel Abe, Sunny Kamahele and Jim Kaupuiki. Sunny had played with us in Hollywood while we were doing some of the television broadcasts for Harry Owens. We did a lot of rehearsing for that record, but it was a lot of fun.

"Jimmy Moikeha was the singing star of the Tapa Room at that time. The next year, Danny Kaleikini joined us. We had a great time working together. He had a terrible temper and I used to tell him, 'Danny, don't let those people get you down. Just do your job and ignore them.'"

Danny has his own version of that first experience working with Hilo. Gracious star that he is today, Danny remembers it like this:

"I feel I was very fortunate to have worked with Hilo Hattie. She's such a pro. Guys like us could never learn anything like this in school. The way she handles people, the way she talks to them, her mannerisms—the way they respond to her.

"One thing Auntie Clara taught me was to control my temper. I was young at that time. No matter what people said, I'd hit first and talk later. A couple of times I did that in the Tapa Room. I just thought—I don't need this, get me out of here. It takes a lot of self-discipline, a lot of getting to know people. 'Cause different people have different ways of reacting. Some people don't react at all. You just gotta work hard, then all of a sudden you turn them around and they're smiling."

Danny certainly did learn his lesson. Now a headliner with his own show at the Kāhala Hilton for the past twelve years, he speaks very humbly and sincerely to those of the younger generation.

"I just want to say for the young people that want to go into show business—if you get a chance to learn from the masters, this is a credit to yourself and a credit to the masters. Whatever they come up with, constructive criticism or whatever, take it for what it's worth. I was smart enough to take whatever they had to dish out and put it to good use."

Danny has a marvelous sense of humor and is a very sharp dresser. Looking at a picture of Clara and himself in that famous jumpsuit, he smiles: "It was the first jumpsuit in Hawai'i. I know it was. I had my wife make it. It was brilliant red and bright gold. The girls would whistle, pound the table and say 'Wow, what's this?' Nobody had ever seen anything like it before. It took a lot of guts to wear it. I wore it at the end of the show—when I'd come back to make kanikapila. You know—when Grandma would get up and dance and Grandpa would sing—family style.

Danny wears the first jumpsuit in Hawai'i. (Irene Morton)

"We used to go out to a restaurant after the show—eat family style. It was good. As many shows as they have in town, I think this relationship with everybody is good. If you have differences, you can air them out and that is the time to do it. And you learn. Clara would tell me what I did wrong. Sometimes she'd say 'Hey, you poʻo pakiki.' Poʻo pakiki means very hard head and I had it. You know—it was punch first and talk later. I kind of realized later it's not the golden life. You can sit down and study the situation and find the solution. Clara always came up with some good ideas. She always guided me. She knew I was a hard head."

There were many exciting things happening at the Tapa Room. Exciting people. In 1965 President Johnson called a summit meeting with Prime Minister Nguyen Cao Ky of Vietnam and other important officials. While the conference was going on, the Prime Minister's wife made reservations for a party of thirty at Hilo's first show. She liked it so well she stayed for the second show. Apparently, she reported her enjoyment to her husband, for the next day the Prime Minister arranged through the Secret Service to make reservations for a party of eighty! Some of the guests included Vietnamese Chief of State Nguyen Van Thieu, General Maxwell Taylor, General William Westmoreland, U.S. Secretary of Agriculture Orville Freeman, U.S. Ambassador Averell Harriman, and many more, including Conrad N. Hilton himself.

Christmas Eve was always exciting at the Hilton in those days. Everyone was invited—all the employees, all the guests. Of course, the Hilton wasn't as big in those days. Every balcony would be decorated, and on Christmas Eve, every other balcony would be filled with a celebrity that would perform one number. A spotlight would be focused on a balcony where Clara would sing then it would fade away to be brought up on another balcony where a different celebrity would sing or play. There would be fifteen or twenty performers, each on a different balcony, each doing a different number. It was beautiful.

Fellow workers and guests alike have fond memories of Hilo Hattie and the Tapa Room.

Jay Larrin, popular singer, composer and pianist (composer of the best selling *The Koʻolaus Are Sleeping Now*, and many other successful hits), remembers his first encounter with Clara when he came to Honolulu in 1967. "I was very young and I wanted to impress my relatives from Tennessee. They had just arrived and it was their first trip to the Islands. The Tapa Room with Hilo Hattie was certainly the most impressive place to take them. Someone in the band knew I was a singer and apparently told Clara. When Hilo finished the show, she walked right over to my table and started talking about how wonderful I was, saying things like, 'We're so proud of this young man.' What a diplomat. She was really great. She understood how important it would be for me to have an endorsement like that—from somebody like her. I'm sure she did a lot of things like that. She's probably the most loved person in all the Islands."

Marcelle Balzer, with his lovely wife, Elva, operated a fantastic country-inn-style French restaurant in Kailua called L'Auberge. A whole chapter could be written on this couple and their ingenuity, warmth, food and service as it evolves in this restaurant. In the fall of 1967 though, Marcelle was a maitre d' at the Tapa Room. Just a mention of the name Hilo Hattie brings a smile to his face. "She was the warmest person I have ever met. If there is any one person who portrayed the aloha spirit, it was Hilo Hattie. Her warmth and enthusiasm bubbled when she would meet customer after customer when the show was over. And when she did that *Hilo Hop* number, the rafters would shake from the tumultuous laughter."

Carole Kamamura, a former student, remembers not seeing Clara for over thirty years, then hearing she was playing at the Tapa Room. The year was 1963. "I wanted to see her. Already she was very famous, but I just had to see her. I arrived before she did. When she came in, she walked straight toward me and called me by name. I was thrilled. After all those years. She was always smiling. Always made you feel so good. Whatever her cares, she was always smiling."

Jo Flanders was hired as entertainment director for the Hawaiian Village while Clara was playing there. Jo remembers her first meeting with Clara from a completely different angle. When Jo first met the dancing group that accompanied the show, there seemed to be an air of resentment. One of the girls refused to do a specific number and the dancers didn't want to practice. There was even talk of quitting the show. Clara went to one of the rehearsals and really told the girls they should listen to Jo. "She knows what she's doing, and you should listen. You just aren't used to having fine direction like this. You are used to doing everything your own way and not used to taking orders. Give Jo Flanders a chance." From then on everything went well between director and chorus.

Time after time, someone related how Clara eased tension—what she would say or how she would act funny and make them laugh. "She always had time to listen to our complaints too," one of the dancers recalled.

Benny Kalama often tells about some of the good times they had at the Tapa Room. "Clara always liked to celebrate people's birthday parties. Time after time, we'd have a party after the show. She'd always have a lei or some special gift. I used to call her 'Primo' because she brought so much Primo to those parties. She'd say, 'Hey Benny, have a Primo,' and I didn't like Primo. A whole gang of us used to go to the Golden Duck—some of the guys in the band, some of the waitresses, occasionally even a guest. Sometimes one of the girls had a bottle in her purse to add to the occasion. We had such a good time."

Although Carlyle could not recall the exact date, he is sure that it was soon after John Wayne's first cancer surgery and shortly before Clara's mastectomy that John appeared on the stage with Hilo Hattie in the Tapa Room. And what an appearance—John, who was known for taking an occasional drink, came storming into the Tapa Room with Kim Wai. Before taking his seat he strode up onto the stage, picked up Hattie, embraced her, and then proceeded to explain to the audience just what a privilege it was for them to be entertained by this Hawaiian lady.

One, six feet four, the other five feet—a pair of giants—a gentleman and a lady. They don't make them like that very often.

Clara would do or say anything to make us laugh. (Lily Padeken Wai)

Carlyle and I had so much fun playing at the ʻIlikai. (Carlyle Nelson)

chapter seventeen

The ʻIlikai, Halekūlani, and Other Hotels

On Monday, December 15, 1969, Clara opened at the Canoe House in the ʻIlikai Hotel, back to back with Arthur Lyman. "Playing on a team alternating with a great guy like Arthur Lyman is a thrill in itself. Of course, my own trio was tops with my husband, Carlyle, on steel guitar, also filling in some numbers with the violin or clarinet. Charles Popikala was on guitar and Violet Pahu on bass.

"Arthur was at his finest, and it was fun taking a break to sit in the audience and listen to his show. He combined his job of emceeing and singing along with artful playing of the vibraphone, marimba, conga drums, Chinese chimes, and gongs. His group included Clem Low, Harold Chang, and Archie Grant Jr."

The Canoe House wasn't serving dinner in those days. It was just a nice club atmosphere. Arthur opened first around 9:00 P.M. then Clara would come on. Each did two half-hour segments.

"I remember the first night I opened the show with *Hawaiʻi Ponoi*, singing it from the entrance until I was on stage. The audience loved it. All of a sudden I was smothered with lei and there were tears in my eyes. Then I got all wrapped up in some lively tunes like the *Hilo Hop* and the *Cockeyed Mayor*, and forgot nostalgia for a minute. The *Twelve Days of Christmas*, Hawaiian style, was on the agenda too. It was always so popular at that time of year."

The plumeria trees at their home in Kaʻaʻawa were loaded with blossoms and Clara would often come to work early with huge sacks of flowers. Everyone got busy stringing lei. Even big, handsome maitre d,' Ed Morton, would help.

"Later in the show we'd give the lei to the audience. First we'd honor birthdays or anniversaries, or any special occasion—then, whatever was left, we'd just give them out until they were gone. The audience was so surprised. People weren't used to getting something for nothing, as was our Hawaiian custom.

"We had a room at the hotel, so some nights we would stay in Honolulu. When that happened, the next day, Carlyle would drive out to Ka'a'awa and pick more blossoms. And we'd make more lei."

Each night the show ended with Clara and Arthur singing a duet, *Honey Come Back*. Oftentimes, the audience would join in for a sing-along. Sometimes, Arthur got so wrapped up talking with customers, Clara would get on the microphone saying "Arthur, get your ʻōkole back up here."

Arthur and I would close singing *Honey Come Back*. (Hawaii Tourist News)

In 1970 Clara was still at the ʻIlikai, but later in the year spent a month with Don Ho at the International Hotel in Las Vegas. From 1971 through 1974 she did shows at the Kāhala Hilton hukilaus, the Royal Hawaiian, and Sheraton Hotel lūʻau. Of course, there were a lot of miscellaneous shows, both charity and commercial, between times.

"On different occasions I had the pleasure of working at the Halekūlani Hotel—good ole Halekūlani. What a legend it is. From the time it was first used as a hotel in 1917 to the present, the Halekūlani has offered a very special kind of Hawaiian hospitality. Many magical moments have been stored in sweet memories while dining under the hau trees on the Coral Lanai. It's about the only hotel dining room in the world that regularly carries a cover charge for a happy-to-pay dining crowd on the inside and a non-paying beach going audience on the outside. The entire front of the dining room is open to the beach and the sounds of the surf and an audience from babies to octogenarians are there to enjoy it. I remember Emma Veary always dedicated one number each night to her 'beach audience.'

"In March of 1974 I had the opportunity of filling in for Emma while she was touring Europe and doing a show at the Hotel Savoy in London. The wonderful Kailua Madrigals joined me that year."

Clara loved those Madrigal Singers, and the Madrigal Singers loved Clara. Officially called the "Sounds of Young Hawaiʻi," this group of Kailua High School youngsters, under the direction of Shigeru Hotoke, each summer spread the word of Aloha and the spirit of goodwill by sharing their music, dance, and youthful enthusiasm with the people of the world. This was the fourth year the Madrigal Chorale group had circled the globe. To call them "singers" is a misnomer—they put forth so much talent in their dances and chants. They cover all areas of Polynesia.

Shigeru loves to tell how thrilling it was to work with Clara. "Everyone of our group just adored her. She was all at once a champion performer, a friend, a teacher, and always the 'beloved Auntie Clara.' She was precious to us. Sometimes, she came over to Kailua and performed for us. The kids always listened to her. She would tell them, 'Now you don't miss school and you study.' Her words cut deep. The kids respected her."

On the lighter side, Shigeru also likes to relate how Clara sometimes changed her program without warning. "But the kids fell right into the unscheduled number as though nothing had happened. They knew her numbers so well. I guess all of them were aware of Auntie's great reputation for ad-libbing, and how it would carry her into another song. Of course, Carlyle was always there too. He was such a help with all the music at a second's notice."

In July of the same year, Clara was again asked to fill in for Emma at the Halekūlani. This time the show had a completely different theme. The famous Farden Family was part of the show, and what a glorious show it was. Each of the eleven sisters and brothers did an act. Sometimes it would combine brothers and sisters in an old fashioned waltz, sometimes there would be solos with each person representing a different island, wearing the colors and flowers of that island. The brothers would do the old hulas the men were taught to do before women were allowed to dance. Then, in the midst of all this drama, sister Annie would come out with a whistle that would make the audience burst into laughter.

While the Farden family would have been a show all by themselves, there was much more offered those nights. David Kelii played the steel guitar, Ida Naone danced and then there was Sol Bright, Sr. Sol is a legend in his own right. Classed as a comic, composer, musician, director, actor, producer—there isn't much Sol hasn't done. And done well. This time in addition to his comedy, Sol added a new depth to his singing. Clara had discovered Sol could really sing good bass. "She heard me singing at a musicians' union rehearsal," Sol recalls, "and asked me if I could do *Wili Wili Wai*." I said, "Sure." "You're a basso," she said, "Do that one in the show."

"For the first time that night I performed *Wili Wili Wai* as a basso and it brought the house down. I had known Clara for years, and she had never told me I was a basso before. That gal has some ear for music. She can inspire talent out of anyone."

Amid all that talent, Clara was still the star of the show, and, as usual, thrilled the audience whether she was doing a comic number or a more serious one. On the final night of the three-week show, there was a very emotional climax. Sol started the whole thing by making an announcement that he had a present for Auntie Clara.

"I bought her a big orchid and had it in a box. As you know, our custom of giving lei is very common, but an orchid in a box is something different. I tried to give it to her three times, and she kept pushing it away. 'No—no—I don't trust you,' she kept saying. Finally I took it out of the box and as I was pinning it on her, I started singing the beautiful song, *An Orchid For You* (written by Mack Gordon and Harry Revel). The song is not a very popular one, but the words were so appropriate.

> For your wonderful smile, an orchid to you./For your beautiful eyes, an orchid to you./It's plain to see that you are heaven sent and finding you, my dear, was a blessed event./For your marvelous smile, an orchid to you./For your kissable lips, like petals with dew./My song of love is ending, ending dear by sending, a great big orchid, a great big orchid, to you.

And then every member of the cast came forth offering the beautiful lei they had been wearing all through the show."

And once again the audience was blessed with a Hilo Hattie special that can never be repeated.

In 1975, Clara did another show at the Halekūlani, this time with Sol Bright, Leinaʻala Heine, a comic dancer-singer, and the Madrigal Singers. The Madrigals performed one week; the second week The ʻAiea Swinging Singers, another excellent high school troupe some forty strong, did the show.

The Ala Moana Americana Hotel was featuring Al Harrington that year, and when Al had to go to the Mainland, Clara was asked to fill in as star of the show. Kimo Kahoano was emcee at that time and what a marvelous job he did! In addition to being one of the top disc jockeys at Hawaiʻi's leading Hawaiian radio station, KCCN, Kimo is also a marvelous dancer. Watching Kimo dance songs like *Laupāhoehoe* is thrilling.

Kimo likes to remember working on that job with Clara. "It's easy being young not to realize what a person has come through to be what they are. It's easy to assume that things just happened yesterday. Being involved at KCCN radio, to me, she had always been Auntie Clara of the recordings. Now, here I was as emcee and working live with her on stage. It was thrilling. She was a lot more mellow, but in the same respect, she was very special. Always very clear and articulate. She always performed with so much confidence and people liked that. Being in show business for so many years, she saw a lot of things pass and a lot of people passing, but she never changed her ways. Auntie Hilo always told me, 'Just do your very best, and people will love you.' The first time I ever worked with Auntie Hilo was at an ASTA convention in Seattle in 1962. She was the star of the show and I was just a dancer. I never really got to know her, like I did here at the Ala Moana."

On Monday, January 3, 1977, at age 76, Hilo Hattie once again entertained at the Halekūlani. It had been two years since Clara's last appearance here and the audience was filled with emotional anticipation. No better words could be found to describe that opening than those of the brilliant entertainment editor of the *Star Bulletin*, Pierre Bowman. With his kind permission, here is an excerpt from the way he reported opening night:

> Love, affection, warmth—three words. Three inadequate words. And add nostalgia. Also inadequate.
>
> They are the words one gropes toward, trying to describe Hilo Hattie, who is the newest thing on the nightclub scene in the new year, as well as one of the most venerable legends of entertainment in the Islands.
>
> Last night she opened at the Halekūlani Hotel, and her performance is a fragile feast, pulling at memories of years past, putting an audience in a peculiar state of bliss.
>
> As Hattie performed, women at ringside covered their eyes, and sweet tears streamed down faces lined like fine old linen. One woman wept openly, her body heavy with sobs...

> ...She is, all at once, today and yesterday, all wrapped up together, the innocence and naivete of days past when things seemed more simple and more fun, right up there, right now, proving, if only for an evening, that the yesterdays are not lost forever...

This year, Elmer Ke's orchestra was playing at the Halekūlani. It was a quartet consisting of Elmer, Benny Kalama, Norman Isaacs and Harold Chang. Carlyle accompanied on the violin. Clara's partner in entertainment was a new find she had discovered while doing a brief engagement on the island of Kaua'i—a 16-year-old 'ukulele player named Dean Guzman.

Dean Guzman was a student at Damien High School and had been playing the uke since he was six. He had a natural flair for it. His timing and improvisations were magnificent. Dean was scheduled to do three numbers each night, but the audience clapped and clapped so much, he ended up doing six or seven.

"Backstage he told me how thrilled he was to be performing with me—as a soloist—and at the Halekūlani. I in turn told Dean how thrilled I was to be playing on the same show with him.

"I'll never forget the last night of our performance. Our show concluded with the usual finale with Dean and I doing a number and exiting together while the lights faded out. Over the loudspeaker came an announcement, 'Auntie Clara. Dean has a special surprise for you.' I couldn't imagine what surprise I could be getting from this wonderful 16 year old. He went out on the stage, sat down with this uke, and proceeded to play *When Hilo Hattie Does the Hilo Hop*.

"Needless to say, I was choked with emotion. When my heart fills up with so much pride, my eyes uncontrollably start watering. Of course, I just had to get in there and do a little hop. Just couldn't miss an occasion like that."

And once again, the audience was treated to an exclusive special that is part of the Hilo Hattie scene wherever she goes.

Dean did not play along with the orchestra on any of the Hilo Hattie numbers. Later, Clara learned he had started practicing the *Hilo*

Hop number at home, after the first night of the show. Unbeknownst to anyone, he kept practicing until that final show when he made his magical presentation.

"I might add," said Clara, "He put a couple of chord changes in that song I had never heard before. Another sweet memory."

Randy Lee, manager of the Halekūlani Hotel, is proud of adding this segment of entertainment to the Coral Lanai. "She epitomized all the things that are the essence of Hawaiian entertainment, and so we contacted her to ask if she would do a show," Randy said, as he mused over their first person-to-person meeting. "Clara said she was so flattered to think at her age, when most people would be retired, that there was some place she could share her talent and that it would be appreciated. She also said she felt so fortunate to be given this talent."

Randy goes on to explain that their relationship was a complete love affair from the time they first started working together. "Every moment she spent in this hotel, she added something to our lives. She is the most gracious lady I have ever met. She gives so much to others. Age was never a factor. She has energy. She has enthusiasm. She has a childlike quality that captured the hearts of others. She has a God-given quality that is rare to find. It is regrettable that today's entertainers do not understand what commitment is. Clara has it all."

The Kailua Madrigal Singers are wonderful. (Halekūlani Hotel)

Love that Hilo Hattie Paradise Cake. (Allan Hunt)

chapter eighteen

A Flirt with Business Adventures

"When you're in middle life, sometimes your mind reflects on venturing into the business world like you read about in *The Wall Street Journal* or *Newsweek*. Show biz has always been our business world. Every once in a while, Carlyle and I would sit out on the lanai enjoying the peaceful view and discussing possible financial aspects of the future.

"Nothing much happened.

"Then one June day in 1969 an energetic young advertising executive came to Honolulu with a gleam of an idea—to make cakes or confections that would carry a famous Hawaiian name. His first thought—Hilo Hattie.

"Carlyle was, and is, the financial wizard of the family, so when Allan Hunt phoned that day, I turned the call over to Carlyle."

Allan recalls, "Yes, Carlyle was with the Royal Hawaiian Band and they were playing at the 'Iolani Palace Bandstand the next day at noon. He asked me to meet him there before the performance.

"At that time, I was thinking of creating a mail order business with a line of Hilo Hattie products. My first thought was of cakes or confections as pure and sweet as the lady herself.

"Our conversation was brief that day. I tossed out a few ideas of products to consider—a cake using Hawai'i's sweet pineapple and delicious macadamia nuts, some candies—perhaps a fudge with the macadamia nuts. I had never heard of that. We talked a few minutes, then Carlyle suggested I come out to Ka'a'awa the next day and we'd get down to more basic facts."

The next day at Ka'a'awa Carlyle asked, "How many products are you thinking of?"

"Oh, three or four to begin with," Allan replied. "Are you limiting it to edible items?"

"No. Not necessarily. I thought perhaps some Hilo Hattie stationery, and perhaps a booklet with Hilo Hattie telling how to speak Hawaiian."

Clara interrupted. "When you want to add something new to the line, will we have a chance to approve it?"

"Absolutely," Allan replied. "I would only want the very best to come out with the name Hilo Hattie on it."

"We then discussed the financial agreement, and I left their home in Ka'a'awa with the feeling that a new business was about to emerge which would be a source of pride and joy to all of us."

The first product to come on the market was a cake using fresh Hawaiian pineapple and macadamia nuts. The first time Clara tasted it, she commented, "This is Paradise Cake." And so the first product in the Hilo Hattie line became "Paradise Cake," which is its name today.

"We tried several products in the next few months," Allan recalls. "Clara's favorite of our next edible line was a product called Hula Corn. It was macadamia nuts covered with a variation of a caramel sauce. Delicious—but between production and ingredients, it turned out to be too expensive to market with much success.

"After the Hula Corn we created a very different recipe for Kona Coffee Candy. It's a hard candy, individually wrapped, and a very popular item on the market today. Our next experiment was with macadamia nut fudge, also very successful on today's market. Then there were Kona Coffee Royals, with a rich creamy center and our latest product, Kona Coffee Thins, produced in a variety of pastel shades.

"We also created a line of Hilo Hattie stationery, as well as a small booklet entitled *Fun and Easy Hawaiian*, as taught by Hilo Hattie. It's an informative little booklet, giving a brief history of Hawai'i, answering the questions most frequently asked of Hilo, and including a brief dictionary of the Hawaiian language, if one can use the term 'dictionary' in a mini-meaning."

The next dabbling into outside business adventure happened in Hilo when Clara went there in 1971 as honored guest at the Merrie Monarch Festival.

A young enterprising couple by the name of Evelyn and Richard Margolis manufacture a very fine line of Hawaiian clothing in their Evelyn Margolis Garment Factory. "We named it that," says Dick, "because Evelyn designs all the styles."

The Margolises are very active in community affairs and were very active in the Merrie Monarch Festival that year. Richard remembers the night vividly.

"The first evening we met, we took Auntie Clara and twelve members of the Hawaiian Civic Club, who were participating in the Festival, to dinner.

"After dinner, we were strolling through the Kaiko'o Mall where we have a retail store. I was explaining that our line had an excellent reputation on our island, but that we were not known on the other islands. Suddenly, I had an inspiration. With your name and our product, we could become an instant success, I kept thinking. Suddenly, I said it out loud."

Clara was surprised. "I don't know. Over the years I've been approached by many people for the use of my name. I've spent so many years making it a good name and I want to keep it that way." As she examined the line more closely, she said, "How much would it be worth?"

I pulled a figure out of my hat.

"All right."

"Have your attorney draw up the papers and we're in business," I said.

"No—you just have your attorney draw up the agreement, and we'll sign it. Carlyle always handles the business end."

"And so we met and instantaneously merged into a new business venture. It has been a lovely association. Clara has gone to several trade shows with us. The biggest was in 1976 at the Hyatt Regency Hotel in San Francisco. There were over 600 different lines from different manufacturers. With the presence of Hilo Hattie, and she did come down daily to play her ‘ukulele and sing, we enjoyed the biggest reputation of any of the manufacturers showing. That was the year Evelyn received the California Designers Award of the Year, under the Hilo Hattie label.

“The last night of market week, salesmen and manufacturers put on a tremendous dinner and show for more than 700 people. As usual—Hilo Hattie was star of the show.”

Then someone mentioned “Hilo Hattie Travel Tours.” With Clara’s love for people combined with her knowledge and love for Hawai‘i—it sounded like a natural.

For a brief time, Clara conducted tours on her own. She went to Hilo, met the airplane and greeted everyone with fresh lei. Then she joined them at the hotel for a little more merriment, explaining what would be going on the next couple of days. There were things scheduled day and night. It was a hectic schedule. Clara soon learned that entertaining a hundred or so, elbow to elbow so to speak, was quite different from being up there on stage seven nights a week. There were always the late risers who didn’t want to get out of bed, the head count every time they got in and out of the bus, not to mention the late-to-bedders who sometimes had a little too much to drink.

And so the venture into “Hilo Hattie Travel Tours” was short-lived.

Carlyle remembers they even dabbled in the ceramic field at one point. “We thought it might be interesting to make a souvenir item—perhaps an ashtray modeled from the famous Hilo Hattie battered hat. We made several thousand of them. At times, when Clara thought there were too many bald heads to kiss, she would hand out ashtrays! In fact, it seemed we ended up giving more ashtrays away than ever found their way into retail stores. So that, too, did not turn out to be a profitable venture.

“And now, Clara and I sometimes sit out on the lānai, enjoying the peaceful view, and not discussing the possible financial aspects of the future.”

Clara teaches visiting statesmen the hula. (Hawai'i State Archives)

My first broadcast was with the *Harry Owens' Show.* (Carlyle Nelson)

Center: Harry Owens
First row (left to right): Napua, Clara, Gil Mershon, Moana, and Lei Aloha.

Second row (left to right): Frank Sabetella on piano, Sonny Kamahele, Prince Kawohi, Ray Carroll, and Mac McGraw.

Third row (left to right): Eddie Bush on steel, Sam Koki, Ole Oleson, Carl Holting, Len Ingoldsby, Jack Narz, announcer.

Top row (left to right): Carl Allen on bass, Glenn Redmond, and Bill Schnutte.

chapter nineteen

Television

Clara's first experience on television was with the *Harry Owens' Show* in 1949. The program was broadcast from the Aragon Ballroom at Ocean Park, California—not exactly a modern, plush television studio. While couples continued dancing, an extra battery of lights would be focused on the band during the one hour show with other spotlights on special performers.

There were no dressing rooms. Applying makeup or changing clothes had to be accomplished in the two restrooms. The men in the band said they felt very silly standing there patting on pancake makeup while customers came in to use the restroom for its more normal facilities. While several members of the band had receding hairlines, Eddie Bush was the only "bald head" that created a problem for the director. It actually made a shiny spot on the screen. For the first broadcast Eddie finally covered his head with eyebrow pencil. It wasn't long before he decided a toupee was the only way to go.

The *Harry Owens' Show* continued on the air for nine years. There were many other impromptu television appearances through the years—with Art Linkletter and Bob Cummings from Los Angeles—with Patti Page from New York. Pearl Bailey also appeared on the *Patti Page Show* at the same time. Pearl asked Clara to join her on the road, but previous commitments prevented Clara from accepting.

Hawaiian television opened its arms to Hilo Hattie's charms on many occasions.

First there was working with Jack Lord and crew in *Hawai'i Five-O*.

"I just had a bit part, but it was a new experience. First I was Mrs. Kapali in 'One Day We Will Be Strangers In Our Land.' The scene on the porch was very emotional. My son was accused of being a murderer. I cried and cried, saying, 'My son is a good boy. My son is a good boy. He did not do that.' The part was so vivid in my mind I couldn't forget it for weeks after the shooting was finished. Two years later they asked me to play the part of Mrs. Pruitt in 'The Late John Louisina'."

Clara always played her parts so realistically, her directors often referred to her as "One Shot Hattie."

After the first filming, Clara was so happy with the entire crew she wanted to do something for them. Finally, she decided to invite the crew to dinner at the Kāhala Hilton where she was performing at that time. Since Clara was in the show and couldn't be hostess for the dinner, she asked her good friend, Jo Flanders, to be hostess for the evening.

An interesting incident arose from Jo's role that night. Jo Flanders was, and is, a very prominent figure in the entertainment field of Hawai'i. One of the staff members at the dinner party asked Jo to stop by the *Hawai'i Five-O* office. When she did, they informed her they wanted her to play a role in their next filming. At first Jo was reluctant to take the part, saying she was not an actress. But they insisted. "Yes, you are just the type of person we want for this particular role." There were eight different women hired to play roles in a mysterious murder plot. Jo appeared on the set per schedule, and was promptly paid per agreement. Anxious to see herself on *Hawai'i Five-O*, Jo kept checking to find out when the program was going to be aired. When she found out the day, Jo dashed home from another appointment to watch the show… only to find out she never appeared on the screen. Six of the other women never appeared either. So much editing had been done, only one of the eight original ladies appeared in the scene. Jo laughs to this day about her famous role on *Hawai'i Five-O*, but quick to add, "But I got paid for it."

Then there was the nationwide hookup of *Mele Hawai'i* on Channel 11, KHET. It featured Clara doing the *Cockeyed Mayor of*

Kaunakakai, and *When Hilo Hattie Does the Hilo Hop*. The same program featured the composers of the two songs, R. Alex 'Andy' Anderson and Don McDiarmid Sr.

On the same station, Pau Hana Years honored Clara on her 70th birthday with surprise guest stars Danny Kaleikini, Sonny Kamehele and Pua Alameida, who worked with Clara through the years.

Doing the *Mike Douglas Show* from the Hawaiian Regent Hotel in Honolulu was another highlight in Clara's television experience. The timing was perfect. Clara was recovering from an endarterectomy. Already she was getting restless, and this was an opportunity to do her act, but not under a rigid schedule of every night at one of the hotels. It was a perfect trial period to see how she could tolerate performing under bright, hot lights. She felt fine. "It made her feel so good," Carlyle recalls. "Now she could be her same old Hilo Hattie self."

Several times Clara was asked to be a guest on the Don Ho Show. A series of shows were broadcast from the Reef Hotel in Honolulu. Clara would always do one song number, then usually a comedy routine about some of her relatives. She often explained how her Chinese cousin got a strange name like 'Ole Olson.' "When Sam arrived from China, he went through the immigration office following a large family of Olsons, the last one in front of him being named Ole Olson. When the immigration officer asked my cousin his name, he replied, 'Sam Ting.' The immigration officer understood him to say 'same thing' and registered Sam as Ole Olson."

Certain segments of the show would have Clara giving advice to the audience on any of their problems. There was the time a young gentleman stood up to ask advice on his problem. "My wife has taken up painting, and did a nude picture of me which she wants to hang in the living room. I would be so embarrassed to have any of our friends see that picture. What can I do?" Clara ponders. "That's hard. A nude picture, eh? That depends which side you were facing. Tell her to add a three leaf clover where it's supposed to be. But if you're facing the other way, she better make it a four leaf clover."

Then a beautiful lady in a strapless sundress stands up. "Do you think I should improve my bust line?" Don Ho is quick to respond that he probably would be the best judge of that. Clara is equally quick to respond. “Improve your bust line? Of course, you should. I did. Now I take the No. 52 bus from Kahuku to Kāne‘ohe, then I take the No. 18 bus to Kailua, and then I take the No. 9 bus to Honolulu, and then I take the No. 2 bus to the Don Ho Show.”

Then there were other segments that showed pictures of Clara and people from the old days with Harry Owens’ orchestra—even pictures of the time she played with Don at the Hotel International in Las Vegas.

Television has been a prominent part of the American family life since 1941, and Clara’s participation since 1949 has added much joy to that American family life.

Just couldn't teach those birds to sing *The Cockeyed Mayor.* (KHET, Channel 11)

I crossed my eyes so many times doing *The Cockeyed Mayor* I went to a doctor to ask if my eyes might stay that way. He said it was the best exercise I could give my eyes.
(Carlyle Nelson)

chapter twenty

Clara the Comic

Although Clara can sing serious songs and has taught many serious songs, unquestionably most of her fame came from being the comic, plus the magnetism of her charm. Her routines of the *Hilo Hop*, the Japanese takeoff on *Shinano Yoru*, and the *Cockeyed Mayor of Kaunakakai* have brought tumultuous laughter to thousands in cities and towns throughout the country.

She had a classic way of telling stories. At some point during a story, she used every part of her body—the hands, the eyes, the feet, the shoulders, the ʻōkole. When she'd tell a two or three part dialogue, she usually assumed the position of each of the characters. In one of her favorites—Murphy in the hospital with a broken leg—she laid on the floor with a stiff leg in the air, telling his story; then she jumped up and assumed the position of the nurse taking his pulse; then pulled up a chair and went into the dialogue of a visitor. When broken-legged Murphy spoke again, Clara was back on the floor with her stiff leg in the air. Her accent for every dialect was superb. Asked by a Jewish couple how she developed such a perfect Yiddish accent for *Becky, I Ain't Coming Back No More*, she explained that, while she had performed this song for years, one night at the Royal Hawaiian Hotel she was invited to the table of a wonderful Jewish couple from New York who had enjoyed the song tremendously. "They patiently spent over half an hour with me perfecting the accent."

But there's a comic side of Clara, which is just her natural way of life. Clara is Clara and that's what everybody loves. Thousands of philosophical words have been written on how to attain happiness—of learning to be YOU and loving that YOU. This philosophy seems to have been born in Clara.

❊ ❊ ❊

Beryl Bass, a friend of Clara's since 1933, loves to reminisce about the "good ole days." Her face lights up and she downright bursts into laughter. "I remember the time we were walking along Fort Street and Clara's half slip started to fall down. We were right in front of McInerny's Department Store and Clara just kept right on walking until one foot was out. Then she kicked the other in the air, with the slip going against McInerny's window. She grabbed it, folded it over her arm, and we kept going just as though nothing had happened. I would have been embarrassed to death! Clara was such great fun. It made you feel good just to be with her."

Beryl goes on to recall the songs she used to sing with Clara. "Clara taught me to sing *Koni Au* (commonly referred to as King Kalākaua's drinking song). I used to sing it at parties and the Hawaiians would laugh and laugh. I never found out till years later she had taught me some naughty words!"

❊ ❊ ❊

After completing the Royal Hawaiian Hotel engagement, the famous bandleader, Chick Floyd, opened at the Mural Room of the Hotel Baker in Dallas. To his delightful surprise, MCA (Music Corporation of America) had signed Hilo Hattie to be his headliner. Benton Baker was the owner of the hotel. Chick recalls, "This was in December during the Christmas season, and Benton kept warning us not to be discouraged if there weren't many people in the audience, 'cause December's always bad, with people shopping, parties and families. At that time we were doing three shows a day—lunch, dinner, and supper. The first day we opened, we were packed and Benton just couldn't believe it. 'Must be because of Hilo Hattie,' he said.

"After a week of three shows a day, Benton asked if we could think up something different for the third show. We were repeating the same show as the first one. I told Clara what Benton had said. That night, Clara gave me a wink, and a come hither glance. 'Quick,' she said. 'Let's change costumes.' I was wearing a white suit, shirt, tie, coat—she was wearing her mu'umu'u, the hat, the lei—the whole business. I didn't have to play the piano for this number because it was orchestrated for the hula. We switched our clothes in two or three minutes. We had to, 'cause the hula dancers were coming off the stage. We walked back on the stage as though nothing had happened. Clara kept going and sat down at the piano and I stayed on stage and started doing the hula. The band about cracked up—the audience too. From that time on, our third show was packed 'cause the audience never knew what Clara or Chick would dream up."

❊❊❊

Clara always "talked" to her audience. Many times when the girls were dancing, she described their movements. Her monologue was never the same. She read her audience and played back according to her feeling. A typical number might have gone something like this: "If there is one in the room that is a visitor to Hawai'i for the first time, I'd like for you to enjoy your stay a little better by trying to explain some things we do in our kind of entertainment.

"Some of the things we do need an awful lot of explaining.

"I say this because some of the responses we get sometimes—especially while the girls are doing the hula and the girls are swaying here and there all over the place. There'll come a voice from the audience, and it's always a man's voice, shouting 'Take it off, take it off, or shake it up.' And this isn't that kind of dance.

"The hula is a descriptive dance. It's lovely. And we tell you a story. And we describe the story with our hands. The rest of the movements are added to make it more graceful. So we tell you to 'keep your eyes on the hands.' I catch more guys watching the wrong places all the time. That's why I keep harping on it. When we sing about a little grass shack, we build the roof of a little grass shack (always demonstrating as she is talking). For a stately palm tree, we plant one, straight and tall. We always give it a little soil and a little rainfall. And then sometimes you get this motion at the wrist. That's when we're singing about the tradewinds that blow gently. If it's a strong wind, it's always this big motion over our heads.

"Now, we have a little fish in the Islands. It's about that long. (She shows the size between thumb and fourth finger) and it's called *humuhumunukunukuapuaa*. We have a fish this big (stretching her arms very wide), and it's called the *ono.* (Audience always laughs.) But no matter what size, here's how to make a fish. Extend your arms with the fingers close together. Put one hand on top of the other, extending the thumbs. Let the fish go in and out of the water. (She walks across the stage.) Ideas like these we put to music and we do the hula. So remember now—keep your eyes on the hands. Maybe you don't want to know the song—then you don't have to keep your eyes on the hands."

❊ ❊ ❊

In her version of *Shinano Yoru*, a very popular Japanese song, Clara actually transformed herself from the Hawaiian comedienne to a Japanese geisha right on the stage in front of your eyes. After chatting a bit in broken Japanese, she went on to explain that geishas take about four hours just to put up their hair into a pompadour style. "It won't take me that long, 'cause I don't have much hair. On top here, they wear a headgear which is very colorful and sorta boxy, which I don't have, so I'll borrow some drum sticks." After placing those in position, she commented, "They better not see me at Cape Canaveral. They'd probably send me up."

While Benny Kalama played Oriental background music, Clara announced the name of the brand new composition they played—"*Will they put the auditorium in Diamond Head?* by Benny Kalama and his Nagasaki Syncopaters."

From Hawaiian comedienne to a Japanese geisha for *Shinano Yoru*. (Lily Padeken Wai)

She continued dressing. "They wear a very lovely kimono and it's very expensive. This is a very plain everyday one. Did you know they wrote a song for the kimono? It's called 'Kimono my house'! They also wear a pad on the back. It's held up by a sash they tie very tight. This is also of oriental design and very expensive. I use a hotel towel. It gives the same effect!"

She explained hearing this haunting Oriental song at many of the Air Force Bases visited while on the Mainland. I asked what the name was and they told me, "She Ain't Got No Yo Yo." The Japanese name is *Shinano Yoru*. I don't know the words, and just a little of the tune, but I'd like to do it for you."

She continued singing her version, which is very comical. Words cannot describe this hilarious production with Hilo Hattie's antics and Benny Kalama's Oriental music.

❊❊❊

Everyone in the show knew that Clara loved Chinese food and that she was an expert in ordering, no matter what town we were in. After the show one night in Portland, Oregon, the whole gang decided to go for some Chinese food at a little restaurant they visited quite frequently. Johnny Kaaihue didn't actually speak Chinese, but he liked to mutter a few mixed up phrases with a few Chinese words now and then. Sometimes his muttering seemed to irritate the Chinese waiters. This night, two of the waiters listened to Johnny for a few minutes, then disappeared, and no one was seen for another twenty minutes. They were all sitting around the table wondering when they could order when all of a sudden, here came these two waiters with huge trays of food. They started placing the dishes on our table when Clara asked, "Who ordered that?" "Him order, him order," replied the waiters in unison, pointing their fingers at Johnny. Being the good sports they were, they divided the bill nine ways, kidding Johnny all the time that they should make him pay for the whole thing.

While they were playing at the Mural Room in the St. Francis Hotel in San Francisco, Prince Ernie Kawohi was a very popular member

Prince Kawohi and I used to do a comic hula on stage. One night his zipper broke and you should have seen him trying to do the hula with his legs together. (Bishop Museum)

of the band, playing guitar, singing and dancing. He was very charming and considered quite a ladies' man. The Saturday afternoon tea dances were quite the social event of the era. In fact, your social status was labeled by where the maitre d' placed your table. Clara laughed and laughed as she remembered playing a joke on him at one of those tea dances.

"I wrote Ernie a note explaining that I was dying to meet him and that I would be at next Saturday's tea dance. If he was interested, please put a white carnation on his guitar."

Next Saturday afternoon, sure enough, Prince Kawohi walked up to the bandstand, crisp in his sharp white uniform, his shoes polished to the hilt, with a big white carnation on his guitar. Everyone in the band knew about the joke and couldn't keep from grinning as Ernie kept looking over the room to see if he could recognize the lady. The lady never showed up. That week, Clara sent him another note, apologizing for not being able to come that Saturday, but she could make it the next Saturday for sure. If he was still interested, put another white carnation on his guitar.

Sure enough, there came Prince Kawohi with another big white carnation pinned to his guitar. Kawohi looked over the audience with every note he played, and the band about cracked up. Finally, somebody in the band told him it had been a joke, and he about killed us—Clara in particular.

❊ ❊ ❊

Clara wasn't the only comic in those traveling days on the road. Frank Sabatella likes to tell about the last trip from Los Angeles to San Francisco back in 1950 when they were making those Sunday flights to televise the Harry Owens' weekly show from that area.

"The trip always lasted one hour and fifty eight minutes, give or take a few, in our chartered DC-3. As soon as the plane would take off, we'd all get out of our seats, settle around the big bass drum and start playing poker. We never strapped in in those days.

"One of the guys in the band, Carl Holting, we often referred to as the human garbage can. He ate everything in sight. If he couldn't eat it right then, he'd stuff it in his pocket. That's the way it was on every trip. This return flight was very rough—the roughest I'd ever experienced. Everyone was feeling queasy. Finally, an announcement came over the speaker that everyone should get back in their seats. It was expected to get rougher. Carl was holding his stomach, then his head, and muttering some uncomfortable sounds. The plane had no airsick bags. Needless to say, Carl was first to get sick. He whooped with such gusto it blew Eddie Bush's toupee off. By this time, everyone in our group was vomiting except myself and Harry Owens, who was in the back of the plane fingering his rosary. A hostess came back to see if she could do anything. The stuff was running down the aisle so thick, she slipped, almost fell, but caught herself on the seat, quickly turned and went back to her station.

"As soon as the plane landed, Carl was first off. He dashed down the steps, kissed the ground, and promptly puked again."

Then there was the night Colonel Sanders was in the audience. He too did a graceful hula. After we danced, I kissed him in appreciation. His comment? "If you teach me to do the hula, I'll teach you to cook chicken!" (Honolulu Advertiser)

At almost every performance Clara picked someone from the audience to teach the hula. Often she chose servicemen—frequently sailors. Watching sailors do the hula in those tight pants always made the audience roar.

"I was playing in the Tapa Room one night and I chose a distinguished gentlemen sitting at a table just in front of the stage. He was reluctant to join me. People often reacted that way, so in my usual persuasive fashion I grabbed his hand and helped him on stage. He seemed to walk with difficulty but went through the regular routine and did fine. The audience clapped and clapped. After the show was over, I went down to the table and thanked his wife for allowing me to dance with her husband. 'You don't know how happy that made us,' she replied. 'Arthur has very bad arthritis and he hasn't been able to walk without a cane for six months.'"

While at the St. Regis Hotel in New York, at rehearsal they decided to change the routine on the *Cockeyed Mayor* number. First, the three dancers did a new version of the number and then sat down on stage while Clara entered to do her solo. All of a sudden they looked at each other in surprise—they were wearing all three of Clara's hats. "What is Auntie Clara going to use for a hat?"

Lily Padeken Wai laughs heartily as she remembers Clara's stage entrance that night. "Clara took the lampshade in her room and plunked it on her head for a hat. She proceeded to do the number with the usual smiles, action and song, interspersed now and then with a few Hawaiian words muttered under her breath so that only the girls could hear. 'What do you rascals mean taking all my hats. I'll get even with you later.' The audience never knew it wasn't part of the act, but the girls giggled for many years later when they thought about Clara's appearance in the lampshade hat."

With the usual straw hat missing, Clara substitutes a lampshade. (Lily Padeken Wai)

Lū'au need not to be as elaborate as this. It's the fun, merriment, music, singing, and dancing that make a lū'au.
(Earl DeSilva)

chapter twenty-one

Clara the Gourmet

Food, being a part of the good life, and Clara loving every facet of that good life, has certainly been an interesting part of Clara's good living. Whether it was fish and poi, won ton mein or a good steak, Clara loved it all.

Way back when the girls were first starting with the Royal Hawaiian Girls Glee Club, Auntie Lou would complain about the hotel putting out too much food for them. There were always trays of sandwiches and desserts. "I told them they were going to make my girls too fat!"

Although her notes often refer to having "chop sui—good" or "chop sui—no good," there were many times when they got tired of eating in restaurants while on the road, and Clara or some other member of the troupe would make a special meal.

Lily Padeken Wai, one of Hawai'i's foremost hula dancers who accompanied Clara on her trip to the St. Regis in New York, was Clara's roommate. Lily remembers, "We weren't allowed to cook in our hotel room so Clara would cook on a Sterno stove in the bathtub about three or four in the morning. Clara would say, 'They'll all be asleep now, and won't smell our cooking.' We used to get packages from home. We'd get dried fish and dried squid, cans of laulau or poi. Sometimes there would be fresh poi and what a treat that was. We would stick the dried fish or squid on a fork and hold it over the flame. We had a couple of small pans and we'd heat the laulau in that. We never tried cooking rice though. That would be very hard to do on a Sterno stove. Sometimes we'd just heat a can of soup. We'd get so tired of eating out."

Lily continues, "Clara loved Chinese food. She would even tell the restaurant how to make it. 'Don't put all that gravy on the egg fu yung. A little's OK, but we don't want it swimming in it.' She loved sweet and sour pork and our little Chinese restaurant by Times Square never heard of it. She'd tell them to take some vinegar, brown sugar, soy sauce, a dash of garlic and ginger, and a touch of tomato sauce—and adjust it till it tastes right. It wasn't long before sweet and sour pork became a regular on their menu and that was forty years ago."

One year Marian Manners interviewed Clara for an article in the *Los Angeles Times* with the caption "HILO HATTIE TELLS WHAT MAKES A LŪ'AU." The article quoted Hilo as saying, "Food alone does not make a lū'au. It's the fun, merriment, music, singing and dancing." The article continues on how to decorate your home, with a few recipes and suggestions for getting Hawaiian music, food and flowers.

Irene Morton, a long-time friend of Clara's, recalls the days of the Tapa Room shows at the Hawaiian Village. "She used to bring all kinds of pūpū to eat after the show. I'll never forget those aku bones. She always brought ones with lots of flesh. They're easy to make. Just sauté them in a little oil with a touch of ginger and garlic. The soy sauce is served with them. Sometimes she'd change the recipe and sprinkle some soy sauce over them before cooking."

Several Hawaiian restaurants in Honolulu have aku bones on the menu—sometimes as a side dish, sometimes as pūpū. One of the most popular—Hank's Place on 11th Avenue says they just sauté the bones in oil after rubbing them with Hawaiian salt. "The Hawaiian salt's very important."

Irene also likes to think of the nights they would go to the Golden Duck (now called New Golden Duck) after work. Clara would order won ton mein time after time. Sometimes she'd vary it with saimin. Irene laughs, "We ate so many noodles we thought we'd start to look like a noodle." Benny Kalama and Danny Kaleikini also remember those gabfests at the Golden Duck with fond memories.

Carlyle agrees, "Yes, Clara sure loves her Chinese food. I

remember one time we were on a Canadian tour with the Hilo Hattie show in the small town of Flin Flon. Clara spotted this little Chinese restaurant, and we went in and sat down. Clara proceeded to order in her very efficient Chinese way, without need of a menu. Steamed fish, beef with tomato, sweet and sour pig's feet, won ton mein, etc. The Hilo Hattie show was always famous wherever we went and this little town was no exception. The chef peeked out through the kitchen door to see who was ordering all these fancy dishes—then disappeared. No one came back till what seemed like hours later—but then they presented us with one of the best Chinese meals we have ever eaten. It seemed they had to go out and scour into who knows where, to come up with some of the ingredients, including the fresh fish that Clara wanted steamed."

Clara loves fish and often steams it at home. She always goes to the fish market and makes sure her fish is really fresh. 'Ōpakapaka is her favorite for steaming, with mullet or sea bass running a close second. She steams it the true Chinese way—the whole fish elevated on a rack, sprinkled with oil, a touch of ginger, garlic and green onions. Here's how she makes hers:

STEAMED FISH A LA HILO HATTIE

1 whole fish (2 or 3 lbs.)
1 tablespoon minced fresh ginger
1 tablespoon sherry
1 tablespoon soy sauce
1 tablespoon oil
2 green onion, chopped

Wash and pat dry.

Mix all remaining ingredients except the onion and rub over fish, including the inside. Place on a greased platter and set on a rack in a pan that has a tight lid, with water up to the platter. Steam 15 to 20 minutes, depending on size of fish. Watch for the eyes to become opaque and protrude slightly. Don't overcook. Sprinkle with green onions and serve.

During the road traveling days, Clara always carried a skillet, a couple of kettles and some special "goodies" from home. The troupe remembers with joy the times Clara would surprise them with chicken and long rice. "Sometimes we could buy long rice, like in San Francisco or Los Angeles. I liked to carry a couple of packages with me. It's so easy to make. Tasty and good for you too." Actually the term "long rice" is confusing to some people because it rarely says that on the package. Sometimes it will be called "cellophane noodles" or "bean threads." But we in Hawai'i call it "long rice." This dish holds well and when some of the troupe would be late getting back to the motel, it was a good one to have on the stove.

CHICKEN AND LONG RICE A LA HILO HATTIE

(Some people use stewing hens, but I usually pick up a couple of fatty fryers.)

2 chickens
Water, to cover
2 carrots
2 stalks celery
1 onion
1 package long rice
Salt and pepper

Before cooking, I cut up my chicken for this recipe. Simmer chicken with vegetables until tender (usually about an hour). In the meantime, soak the long rice in hot water for 30 to 40 minutes. Cut in smaller pieces, if desired. Add long rice and simmer another 15 minutes. Some people add soy sauce, but I prefer to let each person add their own soy sauce.

Clara likes spicy dishes too. She loves those tiny semi-hot peppers. Carlyle remembers how happy they were when they planted the chili pepper tree that grows so abundantly at their front door in Ka'a'awa. "Clara would pick five or six of them and put them in her purse when we were going out for dinner.

"I remember at the St. Francis Hotel in San Francisco, there were some miniature pepper trees along the entryway. Clara would eye them longingly every time she went through that entrance. Never picked any though! One year, two of her avid admirers learned of her love for those pepper trees and sent her one for her birthday. She was so thrilled."

Clara was equally thrilled when some member of the troupe would do the cooking. Technically, each was to take his turn, but somehow Clara did the lion's share. Violet Liliko'i traveled with the troupe for several years. She admits she doesn't like to cook. "Love to eat though," she laughs. Several times in Clara's notes, it would say, "Violet bought the groceries today." "Yes," Vi recalls, "I would cook once in a while, but Auntie Clara would help me. Here's how she taught me to make chicken hekka:

CHICKEN HEKKA A LA HILO HATTIE

2-1/2	lbs. chicken, cut up
1	tablespoon butter or oil
1/2	cup chicken stock
1/4	cup sugar
1/4	cup soy sauce
2	tablespoon sake
1/4	tablespoon MSG (optional)
1	cup bamboo shoots
1	cup mushrooms
1	cup shiratake
1	onion
5	green onions

(Some people bone the chicken. I don't!) Sauté till lightly brown. Add next 5 ingredients and simmer 2 minutes. Slice mushrooms, bamboo shoots and onion. Drain shiratake. Add these 4 ingredients to the above and simmer another 5 minutes.

Cut onions in 1-inch lengths, and add just before serving.

"Clara told me there is no set way to make Chicken Hekka. Sometimes we'd add watercress; sometimes we'd leave out the bamboo shoots; sometimes we'd add celery; whatever was around. She used to encourage the one that was supposed to cook to do the shopping. Boy, Eddie Lee used to make a wonderful stew with big chunks of beef and whole onions."

Violet also remembered how thrilled they were when they got a package from home. Clara's sister, Thelma, in particular, would often send them packages. Always there was poi. "Clara would sometimes add cornstarch to stretch it out." Violet remembers too how Clara would make a substitute for lomi lomi salmon, "She'd take a can of salmon, remove the bone, chop it up, add chopped tomatoes, green onion, and Hawaiian salt. We always carried Hawaiian salt with us."

When they were doing the TV shows in Los Angeles with Harry Owens, Clara's husband, Carlyle, would go on to another job, playing for dancing. Some of the other cast had jobs in Hollywood too. Chet Brouwer, then Executive Producer for the show, now living in Honolulu, remembers Clara's cooking with sheer delight.

"Yeah—Carlyle would have to work a dance slot after the show and Clara just wasn't one of those to sit at home twiddling her fingers. Often she would come over to our house. Sometimes she would make sukiyaki. She'd bring it all prepared in nine or ten packages, and a jar of chicken broth. Everything but the soy sauce, that is. We always had soy sauce in the house. She'd squat down in front of the fireplace and cook it in a wok. She'd have it ready in two or three minutes. We were sponsored at that time by Regal Pale Beer, so of course we'd have to wash it down with our sponsor's product!

"Oftentimes we would have to do a personal appearance in a store, and Clara would go up and down the aisles looking for goodies and fresh vegetables. She was so darn cute—sometimes they'd just give them to her. Ah, those were the days." Her recipe for sukiyaki went something like this: (She would vary it according to the icebox.)

For the following recipe, amounts of ingredients are not given because that's the way Clara often cooked. Sometimes if she had spinach she'd add that—or whatever!

SUKIYAKI A LA HILO HATTIE

Oil (sesame and peanut)
Beef, sliced very thin
Celery, sliced very thin
Carrots, sliced very thin
Onion, sliced very thin
Mushrooms, quartered
Water chestnuts, sliced
Bamboo shoots
Chicken broth
Cornstarch
Soy sauce for thickening

Make the oil very hot, add the beef slices gradually, stirring constantly. Remove beef slices. Add vegetables in order listed, stirring well as they are added. "I think the chefs call this stir-fry." Add chicken broth and cook two minutes.

Mix soy sauce with cornstarch—add to above and stir until thickened.

STEW A LA HILO HATTIE

1 can cream of mushroom soup
1 can cream of celery soup
1 envelope dry onion soup
2 lbs. stew meat
3/4 cups wine
Vegetables of your choice

Bake all ingredients except vegetables 3 hours at 300°F.

Add vegetables last hour. "I think cooking vegetables until they're mushy is terrible. If you want to make 'mashed potatoes,' make mashed potatoes."

Sometimes I just felt like sticking my tongue out at 'em. (Carlyle Nelson)

chapter twenty-two

Sometimes Everything's Not Glamorous in Show Business

For the most part, the people Clara worked for were wonderful, as were the audiences. Since all of Clara's numbers were what the motion picture industry would classify as GP, there was rarely an occasion to censor any act. But there were a couple of restrictions that surprised Clara and you might enjoy sharing them.

Becky, I Ain't Coming Back No More was one of her most popular songs, long before *The Cockeyed Mayor* and the *Hilo Hop* were written. Before the war the number would be included three or four times a week when she performed at the Royal Hawaiian Hotel and at the Wai'alae Country Club. After the war, when Clara returned to perform at the Royal—1947, in particular—she did the *Becky* number one night as usual. After the number, she was told by the management that she should not do that number again. When she asked why, Clara was told that a certain *nouveau riche* Jewish gentleman who always stayed at the hotel thought the song was an insult to his race and didn't want it sung anymore.

The next night Clara avoided the *Becky* number. After Clara completed her portion of the show, she sat down at a table in the audience with a customer. The people kept shouting, "Do *Becky.* Do *Becky.*" Finally, she went up to the microphone and made a brief announcement, saying she was sorry—but that she was not allowed to do *Becky* anymore.

The gentlemen who put the ban on *Becky* shall remain unnamed, but the orchestra remembers the ban on *Becky* with a lot of sad memories. The same gentleman gave the orchestra leader a hundred dollars to play a certain number every time he walked into the room.

Princess Pūpūle was another of the most requested tunes in Clara's repertoire. As with most Hawaiian songs, there is usually a double meaning, depending upon the interpreter. The song goes on to say that Princess Pūpūle has plenty papayas and she "loves to give em away." The first time Clara did the number on television, the number was banned.

Agents are a very real part of show business and Carlyle feels they have had a very good relationship with their agents in comparison with some of the stories he's heard from fellow musicians.

For those new, or just coming into the business, you might be interested in knowing that agents work two ways. You can work for the agent, or you can work for the employer. When you work for the agent, he tells you how much you get for the job and pockets the difference of what the employer pays. When you contract with the employer, the employer pays you direct, and you in turn pay the agent his agreed upon commission. For obvious reasons, you must have a reliable agent to agree to the first method.

Carlyle recalls one specific incident when a well-known bandleader was acting as booker for a country club in Houston. "He offered us $400 for a one-night stand. There were nine of us and, obviously, we declined. The next week we had occasion to discuss several one-night stands in Texas with Reggie, our regular agent. The same country club happened to be included for the same date, paying $1,000. Apparently the bandleader thought he could pay us $400 and pocket $600 for his services.

"When I first met Clara, I was appalled at the commission she was paying. When she worked as a single, she was paying 30 percent right off the top. Ten percent to MCA (Music Corporation of America) and 20 percent to Harry Owens. That was the highest I had ever heard of.

"When we first started out on our own, we tried two agents in the Los Angeles area, neither turned out to be very satisfactory. We then found an agent by the name of Reginald Marshall and he really did a first rate job for us. He was taking a flat 15 percent, but he was working hard. He would take out his mailing list, go out and beat the bushes, and cover all the territory in person. He carried his publicity material—the window cards and all that. He was a wonderful agent.

"Lack of communication can sometimes cause hurt feelings too. One day a friend approached Clara on a Las Vegas booking, saying, 'How about if we split the billing and split the profit?' Later, Clara learned he had booked the show without her. 'If he had just called me to say he was doing the show alone and didn't need me, I would have understood. I wonder why he never called me?'

"The only other time a similar incident happened was at the Tapa Room at the Hilton Hawaiian Village. Clara had been having some heart trouble and took some time off. She was asked to come back when she could. 'Maybe you'll be able to come back for the Christmas show,' they said. 'Oh yes, I'll be able to come back by that time, for sure.' During November and early December, Clara kept referring to doing the Christmas show in the Tapa Room. Finally, one day in December, Lani Custino came to her, saying, 'Auntie, I think you should know. We're rehearsing the Christmas show and you aren't in it.' 'Oh?' Clara said in surprise. It was one of the few times Clara registered a big disappointment. 'If they would at least have called me, I would have understood.'

"Going on a job without a contract can become a little scary too. When Clara agreed to do the show in Las Vegas with Don Ho, the agreement included price and time, and all was arranged in Honolulu weeks before the show. No contract ever came in the mail. Clara decided she would go ahead and go to Las Vegas per their verbal agreement. When she arrived, Don's partner decided they could do the show without her. Don Ho, however, insisted Clara be part of the show and at the price agreed in Honolulu. It certainly made Clara proud of Don. She went ahead and started the show without a contract, but a contract did arrive while she was there.

"Ever hear of kickbacks? We rarely did, but it happened occasionally—mostly in the military. I don't know how many clubs suggested it to Clara, but she never paid. There was only one that actually threatened the show. We had a signed contract with the Officer's Club in San Antonio, Texas. The officer of the club called our agent, Reggie, and said he wouldn't let the show go on unless he was paid a fee. Reggie told the officer he would have to let us go on because we had a signed contract. The officer then told Reggie that he would not allow us to go on unless we paid him, and we might as well not show up on the base. Naturally we didn't go, but this one we did report to the Union. The Officer's Club at that base was put on the unfair list and for several months was unable to book any shows. Finally, the Commanding Officer got it all straightened out. They shipped that Club Officer to another post. Clara and I have often wondered if he tried to pull the same stunt at his next post."

Carlyle continues reminiscing on the negative side of show business. "Then there was the episode at the Tropicana in Las Vegas in 1976 that topped them all. At our ages, I don't understand how we got ourselves into a position like that. But then Ken Kaya was taken in too, and he's one swell guy and a damn good business agent.

"Ken operates a contracting firm, along with his wife, Betty, but he manages a few show business people at the same time. There was a booker by the name of Cassini who had booked a show for the Tropicana through Ken. It was supposed to be a big Hawaiian number with twenty to thirty entertainers. Clara was to be the headliner.

"Clara agreed to go. The price was right and they accepted her terms of one month instead of the year they had requested. Ken gave Clara a roundtrip ticket in advance and she left immediately for rehearsals. When she arrived in Las Vegas, the musicians just couldn't play Clara's music. They sent for me to come over and hire some local musicians who could play Clara's music. Ken advanced my ticket also. By the time I arrived, they had hired another group of musicians, that also didn't play Clara's type of music, or perhaps more correctly, Hawaiian music. There were four musicians and four singers. They were excellent in their field. All Negro, they played nothing but rock and roll, opening with 'Aloha' and closing with 'Mahalo'—the only introduction to this supposed-to-be-big Hawaiian Revue.

"By that time they had hired two groups of three dancers each, three from Hawai'i and three from the Mainland—not the twenty to thirty person revue we had been promised in the beginning. We only played one week. Cassini didn't have enough money to pay the cast and the union came in and shut down the show. Our contract called for room and board, but we didn't even get a week of that. In fact, the credit department of the hotel was so furious with the whole show, they wouldn't accept any of my credit cards for the room rent. I tried to explain that I didn't carry that much cash, but they still refused to accept any credit cards. Finally, the manager of the Tropicana interceded and they did honor a credit card.

"We just accepted it as another lesson in life, went down to Bakersfield to see my daughter, and then came home to Hawai'i.

"Royalties on recordings are another questionable item in the music business. The only regular checks coming in have been for those recordings made with Harry Owens. He is very good. We also get occasional checks from the recordings in the Tapa Room at the Hilton Hawaiian Village. It seems some of the others just have a license to steal. It is terrible what they get away with. Just another glimpse of the unglamorous side of show biz.

"Charity affairs and benefits are another area that require caution. Clara has been very generous with her free time for every institution and club imaginable. Occasionally, someone gets overanxious and advertises Hilo Hattie on the program without having asked Clara if she would do it. Usually, Clara would go ahead and perform. Occasionally, when it would actually have been a hardship (like once when we weren't even in Hawai'i), she has refused. In that case, the sponsor simply announced at the time of the program that 'Hilo Hattie wouldn't be able to make it!' I imagine other entertainers have had this experience, too.

"I believe everyone in show business has had a little trouble with the unions at one time or another. We have had very few problems. In Seattle one time we were booked by an agent during a block of time that Reggie, our regular manager, had released. When we arrived in

Seattle, I telephoned the union advising them where we were playing and how much we were getting. They said we hadn't been filed. They did let us play and we paid our taxes without any difficulty. The following day we had a brief appearance in a vaudeville show. Again, I called the union and was told it had not been filed, but they gave us permission to play. Again, we paid our taxes and left for the next stop, which was Walla Walla. While playing at Walla Walla I received a summons from the Federation for a union violation. It seemed a local orchestra had been hired for the entire vaudeville show. They were supposed to play one chord of B flat to open our act and we had opened our act without it. I was fined $25.00 and that's the only fine I've ever had.

"In Norfolk, Virginia, our agent received a letter from the local union which we couldn't quite understand and nothing came from it. Perhaps you might enjoy an exact quote:

> Are attention was call that one of your band Hill Hattie goin to play some engagement in are jurisdiction, one of engagement will take place to night 4/21/60.
>
> Be advice that this is against the Nat'l. By Law Art 17, section 1, if you do not attent this soon we are campell to prefere charge against the said Band (Signed, Treas. Local 125 A.F. of M.)"

Clara performs on a float in the Rosebowl Parade in California. (Bishop Museum)

For a moment Clara weeps when Webley Edwards presents the Nō Ka ʻOi (The Best) Award, then promptly starts doing the famous *Hilo Hattie Hop*. (March of Dimes)

chapter twenty-three

Those Accolades Keep Rolling In

To Clara, the beaming faces of little children, the spontaneous laughter of the audience, the calls for encore after encore—these are the memories that make Hilo Hattie happy and all the credit she needs. But accolade after accolade keep rolling in over the years.

Perhaps the first official and funniest was at the University of Hawai'i Homecoming Banquet of 1939, enjoyed by 300 people, with many more at the dance that followed, Toastmaster Representative Kam Tai Lee presented a humorous skit in which Dr. William H. George, Dean of the College (who, incidentally, had the title "Admiral Sausage") was decorated with the "Order of the Sausage" and Clara was crowned "Queen Bologna."

1949 On January 7, the President, Trustees and Faculty of "Bonehead University of Dallas, Texas" presented a diploma with the notation that "Hilo Hattie had satisfactorily completed the course of study prescribed by the University and has attained remarkable efficiency in juggling the cow's male relatives, and that the University does here and now confer the degree of—Doctor of Spanish Calisthenics." The impressive diploma had 14 original signatures, each with some mighty strange titles such as "Professor of Thermometer Control," "Professor of Garlic Culture," etc.

1951 Hilo Hattie, along with Burns and Allen, won the year's top "TV Performers Woodbury Poll Award."

On August 26 she was made an Honorary Member of the Inner Circle, Press Club of San Francisco.

On November 21, she received a beautiful, colorful, "Certificate of Appreciation" from the A.A.U.N.M.S. by the Potentate of the Al Malaikah Temple" in recognition of outstanding and meritorious service."

1952 Received an award for "Distinguished Service" during the seventeen-hour Celebrity Parade Marathon for Cerebral Palsy.

On August 17, she was given a "Certificate of Merit" from the 32nd District Agricultural Association in appreciation of her outstanding participation in the production at the Orange County Fair.

The same year she was honored with an "Award of Merit" in recognition of her generosity and cooperation in support of the Health, Welfare and Community Services of the Community Chest of Los Angeles area.

1956 On January 31, the Stockton Chamber of Commerce commissioned "Hilo Hattie—Honorary Commodore, Port City of Stockton."

1969 California's orchid expert, Murray Spencer, named a new hybrid orchid the *Hilo Hattie*. Murray recalls the occasion with fond memories. "We were sitting close to the stage. We had had a few drinks or I wouldn't have had the nerve, but when Hilo Hattie stepped down off the stage, I grabbed her hand and asked if I could name a new orchid for her. She looked at me with shock. I continued, 'It has all the beautiful colors of Hawai'i—gold sepals and petals, a bright red lip. 'She smiled her gracious smile and said, 'I'd be honored. As many things as have happened to me on the stage, no one has ever asked if they could name a flower after me.'

"She continued talking to us for a while and my wife, Pearl, was as thrilled as I was. It was a Brasso *Laelia Cattleya*, from the Amber Glow pod plant and the BLC Kong-Urai-Gold. I divided a lot of seeds and shared a lot of them with the World Orchid Society, so there are probably a lot of little *Hilo Hattie* orchids around. I have the one major plant and as long as I live I'm gonna keep that *Hilo Hattie* orchid."

1970 The Hawaiian Music Foundation gave her the HAWAI'I ALOHA AWARD with the following inscription:

> FOR OVER 40 YEARS SHE HAS BROUGHT SMILES AND LAUGHTER TO ALL WHO HAVE SEEN HER PERFORM IN MUSIC AND DANCE. BEING GENEROUS WITH HER TIME—PURSUING THE PROMOTION OF THE TALENTED YOUTH OF HAWAI'I, SHE HAS ENCOURAGED THOSE WITH A FLAIR FOR HER STYLE. THIS FULL-BLOODED HAWAIIAN IS A LEGEND IN OUR TIME.

Time after time, people have called her "a legend." Danny Kaleikini says, "She IS a legend. Auntie Clara is a legend. She's like Diamond Head or the Aloha Tower. I don't care where you go in this world—Hilo Hattie is a legend. When you say 'Hilo Hattie,' people anticipate and they just wait for her. She comes out there and she makes everybody smile. She just knows how to get to the people."

1971 On July 9, the Honolulu Chapter of the March of Dimes sponsored a *Nō Ka 'Oi* benefit honoring Hilo Hattie at Blaisdell Center. It was a sellout house with over 8,000 persons attending. The four-hour show was studded with the best stars. There were winners in different categories including Don Ho, Danny Kaleikini, John Rowles, the Society of Seven, and the Sons of Hawai'i. When Hilo Hattie was named as the first Hall of Fame winner, she was totally surprised and wept. But professional that she is, she quickly wiped the tears from her eyes and promptly did her famous song and dance routine, *When Hilo Hattie Does the Hilo Hop*.

1972 Received the "Salesman of the Year Award" from the Sales and Marketing Executive Association of Honolulu. There was a large luncheon in her honor at the Monarch Room of the Royal Hawaiian Hotel. Danny Kaleikini was the moderator to a sellout audience.

For her birthday that year, United Airlines, also honoring their fifth year of service to Hilo, named a DC-8 Jetliner the "Hilo Hattie." Her comment? "Aw shucks." In October of this year, Hilo was honored on television station KHET. The program, "Pau Hana Years," was televised nationally.

On October 27, a testimonial dinner was given for her at the Kāhala Hilton Hotel. Famous songwriter, Andy Anderson (author of *The Cockeyed Mayor of Kaunakakai*, *Lovely Hula Hands* and over a hundred other songs) wrote a special song for her, *Hilo Hattie We Love*.

1974 (August 21) the Honorable Spark M. Matsunaga entered her in the Congressional Record on Document E 5670. A part of the tribute goes like this:

> "Mr. Speaker, it is difficult to know where to begin in praising the accomplishments of a genuinely sincere and vibrant human being like Hilo Hattie. Her past seventy years of singing and dancing to cheer up the human race have left an endearing sense of warmth, well-being and aloha in the hearts of the people of Hawai'i and all those who have come to know her as an entertainer and beloved *Kama'āina*. She made songs like "Manuela Boy," "The Cockeyed Mayor of Kaunakakai," and "Becky, I Ain't Coming Home No More" famous in her inimitable down-to-earth style."

After additional words of praise and a recap of her history, Mr. Matsunaga continued to quote a lengthy article written by Mary Cooke in the *Honolulu Advertiser*.

1975 Clara had been active in many capacities with the Easter Seal Society since its 1947 inception in

Honolulu. In April, Clara was invited to the Easter Seal Telethon in Hollywood.

"Peter Falk was emcee that year, and when he introduced Hilo Hattie from Hawai'i, she received a standing ovation," reports Dick Peicich, public relations agent for the Easter Seal Society. "And I should know, because I was in the control room those entire twenty-two hours."

In October that year, the Easter Seal Society decided to have a testimonial honoring Hawai'i's famous lady of song, dance and comedy—Hilo Hattie. It was Clara's seventy-fourth birthday and Clara suggested it be a fund-raising event, with all proceeds going to the Easter Seal Society.

The production, held in the Coral Ballroom of the Hilton Hawaiian Village, was called *A Hilo Hattie Love Affair.* Over 1500 attended and the performing guest list was literally a Who's Who log of the entertainment world. Aku, K-59's famous disc jockey and a friend of Hilo Hattie since the early nineteen forties, was emcee.

The program opened with the Royal Hawaiian Band marching in the Ballroom, playing the *Hilo March*. They continued onto the stage, and then played *When Hilo Hattie Does The Hilo Hop*. Of course Clara danced! After a standing ovation, Clara was escorted to a high back rattan Queen's chair and entertained with two hours of song and dance by Hawai'i's finest.

Each person introduced during the program told a story about how Clara had affected his life. In order of appearance, the guest list included Al Harrington, Emma Veary, Danny Kaleikini, Ken Kawashima (Director of Royal Hawaiian Band), Benny Kalama and his orchestra, Jack Lord, Ed Kenny, Beverly Noa, Charles "Bud" Dant, Charles K.L. Davis, Marguerite Duane, Leinaala Heine, Don McDiarmid Sr., and the Kamehameha Alumni Glee Club. After intermission, Brian Keith, Sol K. Bright Sr., Maile Aloha Singers, Irmgard Farden Aluli, Kailua Madrigal Singers directed by Shigeru Hotoke, and Zulu appeared. The program also included film clips from some of Clara's Hollywood movies and *Hawai'i Five-O*.

It was indeed a busy year for Clara's participation in the Easter Seal Society programs.

1978 During August, at the annual dinner of O'ahu's Easter Seal Society for Adults and Children, Clara was named Honorary Member for Life.

And there were many others. Indeed, there are thousands who have given this beautiful lady accolades in many different ways.

Our quiet home in Ka‘a‘awa has the beautiful blue Pacific in the foreground and the beautiful green Ko‘olaus in the background.
(Carlyle Nelson)

chapter twenty-four

The Quiet Years at Our Home in Ka'a'awa

Ka'a'awa is a sleepy little village with the Ko'olau mountains stretching to 1,800 feet in the background and long stretches of sandy beach at the edge of our multi-blue Pacific Ocean. It has no particular historical sites and isn't mentioned in guidebooks. The tourist buses whiz through without giving us a second thought. There are no condominiums or high rises. There isn't even a recorded hiking trail.

The small population (under 900) consists of retired citizens or people who commute to work. There is lovely Ka'a'awa Beach Park, with its excellent picnic facilities, and even a lifeguard station. Kalae'ō'io and Swanzy Beach Parks are also considered part of our area. Kamani, pūhala and coconut palms cover the area, with wild guava and kukui trees on the banks of the mountains.

Our business area is composed of a small post office, where everyone gets their mail in glass-door boxes, the Ka'a'awa General Store, and a small restaurant called Hana's Kitchen, both next to the post office. The most impressive building in our village is the elementary school, which includes kindergarten through sixth grade. If Ka'a'awa has any claim to fame, it might be because of O. A. Bushnell's novel, *Ka'a'awa*, about life in Hawai'i in the 1850s.

In 1960 Clara and Carlyle spent the usual six months on the road and decided to come to Hawai'i for a vacation. Carlyle tells how this became home:

"At first we visited Clara's sister, Thelma. Then friends of ours had a very small place in Ka'a'awa, which they just used for weekends or summer vacations. They wanted to know if we'd like to go out there for a retreat from our busy life in show business.

"That first day we fell in love with the area. In small towns, as many of you know, there's no better place for getting information than the local post office—and that's where I headed the next morning. Edith Yonenaka has been postmistress here for many years. When I asked if she knew of any places around Ka'a'awa for sale, Edith said she thought the one directly behind us on the next street might be for sale. That afternoon Clara and I went to visit the house, which happened to be owned by an old acquaintance of Clara's—Marie Webber. Next day we bought it!

"It was a small house, so we made four additions. The first was to add a large study on the first floor and a huge master bedroom on the second. Next, we enlarged the living room by extending it twelve feet—then a large covered lānai on the front of the house—and finally, another room and bath off the carport. The property is only 13,500 square feet but is contiguous with Government property so it looks larger."

"Another addition of interest has been our bird penthouse. I built it on the top of a ten-foot pole in the front yard, visible from our kitchen window. Every morning, hundreds of birds come to feed."

When they bought it, the landscaping consisted mostly of crotons, which you can still see around the perimeter of the yard. They added hundreds of plants.

At the main entrance they planted a small chili pepper tree because Clara loved those tiny hot peppers. By now it's eight feet tall and produces thousands of peppers. They have several papaya trees, as well as lime, peach, banana, lychee, and macadamia nut. There are flowers too—bougainvillea, bird of paradise, gardenia, lilly, ginger. Their proudest addition is the rose garden.

"Clara loves roses, and while it has been a problem growing roses in this area, ours have done fairly well. I can usually have at least one bud in the house for her to enjoy. We talk much about having a

Of course, we're surrounded by tropical vegetation, flowers, and fruits. (Carlyle Nelson)

vegetable garden and somehow we always seem to end up planting more flowers. Once I tried tomatoes and they didn't do well. Tried carrots too. They had beautiful tops, but were little squiggly carrots. We do have some shallots, garlic, and green onions. The green pole beans have been successful, too.

"Sometimes I don't know if I'm a gardener or a quarry hand. There are so many rocks in the soil you can spend an entire day working and be lucky if you end up with a two-by-two plantable patch. I do have a huge mulch bed which helps," said Carlyle.

"Since we moved to Ka'a'awa our social life has slowed down. We love people and Clara in particular has thousands of friends. But it is just so peaceful, day-by-day goes by, and we just stay home. Time after time, one of us will say, 'Well, tomorrow we'll go out to dinner.' Then tomorrow comes and Clara putters around the kitchen creating a new dish—sometimes for two or three hours. Then we sit down to eat and Clara says, 'Well, I like my cooking.' The biggest affair we ever had was a potluck lū'au for the Hawaiian Girls' Golf Club. We prepared the pig and the main dishes, but every one of those thirty-six girls brought a special dish. It was quite an event with lots of music, laughter and entertainment—by the crowd.

"Sometimes when we're not bird watching, or gardening, or cooking, I go in the study and write a song. Of the trifling songs I have written one started this way: "You've got to stutter just a little when you say Ka'a'awa—more worse yet, our street is Ha'aha'a." The word is not as awkward as it appears because it is really two words: "Ka" means the article "the," and 'a'awa" is a reef fish—the English name for it is wrasse fish.

Reef fishing is still popular. Many set up their poles and settle down for a nap. From the same silly song: "If you like to fish the easy way, set your pole and settle down to stay—tie a string to run from toe to pole. When fish bites your pole will tell your toe."

"Now that Clara is truly slowed down from her strokes, our social life is even quieter. Yet Ka'a'awa has a feeling of peace for both of us. Many people have suggested we take a place in town closer to Clara's therapy. Unhesitatingly, we answer no. Ka'a'awa is home. Ka'a'awa is where the heart lies. Ka'a'awa is peace."

She's wonderful. (Carlyle Nelson)

chapter twenty-five

Carlyle Reminisces

As time winds into the thirtieth wedding anniversary of this wonderful marriage, Carlyle often takes time out to reflect on the good life. Since Clara's major stroke in June of 1977, he has been keeping most of their vast field of friends up-to-date by writing a special report on Clara's progress.

You, the reader, might enjoy sharing exactly what those reports said, and so they are being reproduced in this chapter exactly as mailed.

Carlyle reflects on the homey side, like, "Clara always told me the very first thing she bought with her first paycheck from teaching school was a complete set of silver flatware. Clara and I both had gone through rather one-sided divorces (probably because material things were not that important to us), leaving us with not much in the way of household items. The very first item we bought after we were married was service for two of Wallace Rose Point sterling. We added to it constantly—and use it daily with much delight for both of us. Every time we picked up a silver spoon, it reminded us of our first shopping spree together and the joys we have shared in its constant use."

Reflecting on relatives: "Dad really had a rough time at home. Mother was picking on him all the time, and money was always a scarce item in our household. Clara only knew my father for three years, but I think she shared more love in the brief times we visited him than he had received all his life. One time he was ill, and they phoned us in Los Angeles to tell us about it. He always lived in Visalia, which was 200 miles away. We were quite busy and I said we wouldn't be able to make it up for another week. Clara was working in the yard in coveralls. When I told her about the call, she simply laid down her trowel, said, 'Let's go,' and we jumped in the car and left for Visalia, coveralls and all. A few days before Dad died, we came from San Francisco to see him. He asked Clara to kiss him. She did, and he turned to me saying, 'Ain't she nice?'"

Reflecting on Clara, always a ray of sunshine: "In the summer of 1949 I was playing in Lake Tahoe with Sundays off, and Clara was with Harry Owens in San Francisco with Mondays off. On a dull Monday night, we were playing in a rather dark room to a small crowd, and I happened to have my eye on the door. In walked Clara. Even with her dark complexion and dressed in dark clothes, she seemed to light up the room. Bored musicians and tired customers alike (why do gamblers always look so tired?) seemed to perk up. Clara came up on stage and did one number for us. The whole mood of the room changed. Baby Rose Marie was the star of our show at the time and she and Clara hit it off like old buddies. Rose Marie and Clara have always shared an interest in the Easter Seal Campaign. In fact, Rose Marie even came to Honolulu twice to share in the Easter Seal Telethon with Clara."

July 1977

A note from Carlyle and Clara Hilo Hattie Nelson—with an apology for using a form letter, which means that it will be wholly news to some of your and partly news to others.

On June 15 Clara had a serious stroke. By good fortune, she was with friends, Betty and Allan Hunt, in San Jose. As they are familiar with the doctors and with O'Connor Hospital they arranged for her to have the best of care. After twenty-four days there we came home. United Air Lines with all possible consideration made her trip comfortable. (The sister plane to the one we were on is named Hilo Hattie but it was in Honolulu at the time.) Our daughter Gail came with us and was not only an aid to Clara but kept me from flying somewhat higher than the plane. Gail will have to return to her family in Bakersfield soon. Leina Ala (Babe) Reid is here and plans to stay and help care for Clara when she comes home.

After four days at Kaiser she moved to the Rehabilitation Center of the Pacific, which has an excellent local reputation. Therapy was started immediately. Gail and I were shown the entire operation of the hospital and feel that the attention she is receiving is the very best possible.

Clara's left side is paralyzed. Each day she comprehends more of what is said to her. Although she attempts to respond her response is limited. She is animated, amiable, playful, and sings with me. (While her pitch is less than perfect, rhythm is right on.) She is feeding herself and her customary pleasant stubbornness remains as I have known it for thirty years.

Because the therapy takes all of her strength the doctor says no visitors. As she has more flowers than she can use if you wish to do anything send her a cheerful note. Cards that are humorous make her smile. Gail pins the cards on the drape next to Clara's bed.

I do not really know what to believe in beyond the immediate physical world so I just believe in anything that works. This I ask you—think of the last time you saw her—I'll wager something about it made you feel at least a little bit good. So now smile back at her and if it reaches her it will help—maybe help both of you. Some of you will address her as Hilo Hattie, some as Auntie Clara, and some as Mrs. Sugarplum. (While you are at it Mr. S P could use a smile, too.)

Carlyle

P. O. Box 145
Kaawa, Hawaii 96730
October 24, 977

Report from Carlyle and Clara Hilo Hattie Nelson.

As most of you know, Clara had a massive stroke on June 15. Following her stay in O'Connor Hospital in San Jose, Kaiser in Honolulu, and the Rehabilitation Hospital of the Pacific she came home to Kaaawa and returned to the hospital five days a week for therapy. A seizure sent her back to Kaiser for ten days and she is now home again. To save her the trip for therapists—physical, occupational, and speech, are now coming to the house.

Although progress is slow, progress there is. While the left side remains paralyzed she has recently been able to move the left leg a few inches while lying on the bed. We have both learned to handle the transfers from wheelchair to bed, shower, toilet, and car with no problem.

Communication, while slightly improved, remains extremely difficult. The only time Clara shows irritation is when I just can not fathom her wish. Other than this she remains a beautiful lady in appearance and in spirit.

Clara has always been, in a very personal way, a deeply religious person. Her message to me has always been one that I have found easy to follow—"It is all for the best." And it has been. We have been blessed in many ways. The smallest good deed on our part has been compensated in some manner. At this time we are especially fortunate in having our friend of so many years, Leina Ala Reid, with us. She cooks, sews, cares for the yard and the animals and is a solace to both of us. We have asked for divine aid for little but guidance. Until now, that is. If we may ask for just a little more physical improvement seems a moderate request. Our great plea is for communication. If we could just talk at a simple level, read a little, write a little, do a few crossword puzzles, follow a TV program, what a blessing this would be.

As I watch Clara putting all of her energy into therapy sessions I compare this grand lady, soon to be seventy-six, with some of our sixteen year old vandals who have for all practical purposes given up on living. She will never give up. So even as we now are in our old age we shall fight a good fight and make the best of it.

Clara, who talked and sang so much for so many years, can not say much now, but she can still say "I love you." So can I. And we both say it to all of you who have affection for her in your hearts.

Carlyle

Christmas 1977

Taken at Clara's 76th birthday party.

Taken at home in Ka'a'awa.

Mele Kalikimaka

Something about the climate in Hawaii brings on a song, and that is a fine thing. Because we know that many of you are concerned about Clara's condition following her stroke we decided to bring you a bit of Christmas cheer by writing you a song.

A love song it is—a love song to all of you who have a warm place in your hearts for Clara.

So that you will know how well she looks we brought in some greenery from the yard, put on our newest clothes, and set up our camera.

Of course it isn't all flowers and singing and holiday cheer but for the tough part we are three tough old characters and you count on us to do our very rehabilitating best. Communication is hard but it is improving. The left side remains paralyzed but the left leg is starting to assert itself. Our three professional therapists are fine and we two amateurs have learned a lot.

The encouraging words from so many of you remind us that friends are beautiful and we feel your friendship to be our finest Christmas gift. So a happy holiday to you, a happy New Year to you, and most affectionate greetings from—

Clara Nelson (Hilo Hattie)
Leina Ala Reid (Babe)
Carlyle Nelson

OUR CHRISTMAS WISH FOR YOU
THIS LITTLE MELODY FROM YOUR OLD FRIENDS IS
OUR CHRISTMAS WISH TO YOU FOR LOVE THAT NEVER ENDS.
THIS YEAR WE'VE LEARNED AGAIN THAT LOVE MEANS LIFE. WE'VE
PAID OUR DUES, WE'VE DONE OUR BEST, WE'VE REALLY LEARNED TO FIGHT. THE
HAPPY SPIRIT OF THIS SEASON WE WANT TO SHARE WITH YOU. FOR
YOU WE FEEL WE HAVE A REASON TO WISH YOU ALL A SMILE OR TWO.
WE WANT YOU ALL TO KNOW THAT WE ARE FINE. WE
HOPE THE NEW YEAR TREATS YOU WELL. GOOD LUCK WITH FATHER TIME
GOOD LUCK, GOD BLESS, ALOHA NUI LOA. FROM
AUNTIE CLARA HILO HATTIE MRS. SUGARPLUM NELSON,
LEINA ALA BABE REID, AND
CHIEF WHEELCHAIR NAVIGATOR MR. SUGARPLUM CARLYLE NELSON.

P O Box 145
Kaawa, Hawaii 96730
September 1978

Report on Clara Hilo Hattie Nelson.

Our last report was a Christmas time and I had planned to write another in six months but because we had a set back in April I delayed. An earlier report would have been hard to write.

April fifth was our twenty-ninth anniversary. That night Clara had a seizure and either then or soon after she had a second stroke—hitting the same area as the first stroke but not in as severe manner. In addition to that problem we found that there was a lesion in the liver. The reason that I can write now is that a liver scan has shown that hormone treatments have kept the lesion from increasing in size and also because Clara has been gaining strength and feeling better.

Communication remains difficult and it is hard to take much of an interest in ordinary affairs. However, she enjoys our three cats, the flowers, and greenery in the yard, good food, letters—preferably more about what your activities are than about your concern for her—and visitors. We do a three-handed needlepoint where I hold the material and do the up stroke and she does the down stroke. We are working on a pussycat now. If you remember that cat in the Christmas picture this one is supposed to resemble her. (Miu Lan)

During the times we have worked together I have always been the straight man, but although it is late in our careers we have finally developed a comedy routine, thought of by Clara. In the morning when I transfer her from the wheelchair to the toilet she thought of the word "dance." So now I ask her for this waltz, she consults her dance program and agrees. With our own words to the "Beautiful Blue Danube" it goes like this:

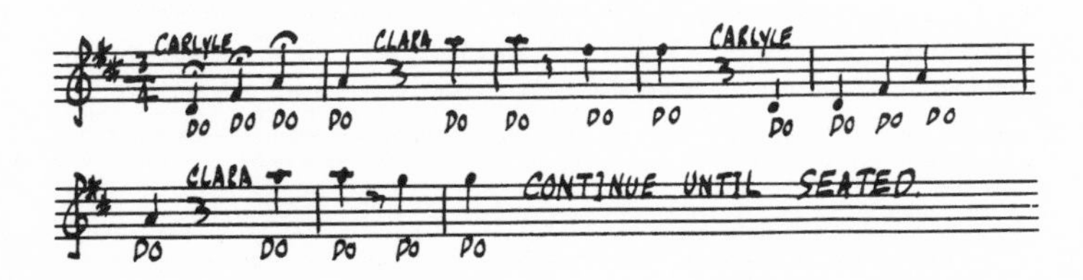

Even though this will never play Peoria I know it will please you to hear that her delightful sense of comedy is still a part of our lives. To have her problems and be as cheerful and affectionate as she is only one of the things that makes this wonderful Hawaiian lady deserving of the affection that you, her friends, feel for her. The mix—friends, affection, hope, good wishes—is beautiful. I salute all of you.

Also your friend,

Carlyle

P O Box 145
Kaawa, Hawaii 96730
December 1978

Report on Clara Hilo Hattie Nelson

The bell in the song has many functions. In appearance an ordinary small cowbell, it seems to have come from the mystics of a different island. You will identify the island by the name of the bearer of the bell—McLenahan. It hangs over Clara's bed where it serves as a call bell. And when you want a bed pan right now a call bell is of prime importance.

Although in illness and in health, in public and in private, we have tried to keep the light touch, we must admit that 1978 has been a difficult year. Of course no one promised us that life would be a fair game and no one promised us roses. But then for most of our many years we have had fun with the game and we do have roses on the table almost every day of the year, from bushes planted by Clara, and each new blossom brings a smile to her lips. Being able to smile at anything with the problems she has had a tribute to her goodness and guts.

Medically probably the least serious of her problems has been a miserable itch. Having no apparent physical basis it is either a work of the devil or of frustration from being inactive. But as I call on the bell for a curse on Satan a rustle of wings followed by a tender voice says "But she lives and there is love, is it not so?"

Medication has reduced the itch considerably. And her medical care is excellent. Her doctor is thorough, has access to the latest in diagnostic gadgets and nuclear cameras, is compassionate, and is compatible with Clara in that he too has the light touch.

Clara's heart has not been good for many years. Three years ago she gave it a boost with a pacemaker. But the pacemaker has its own limits so she recently had to spend twelve days in the hospital with a congestive heart condition. She is home again and her heart is behaving. With the stroke, liver, heart, itch, and communication problems there is much to contend with, but we are strong contenders.

I have finished the year with two awards, one for a musical arrangement that I do not regard as especially good, but with a more meaningful one from Clara's doctor—he says that I am now a fully qualified nurses aid, first class.
If Saint Peter will receive me I shall register as nurses aid doubling on violin.

We'll do our best next year and we shall hope for the best for you.
Aloha no māua is 'okou a pau loa.

Carlyle and Clara

CHRISTMAS BELL
ON CHRISTMAS DAY WE'LL RING A BELL — A
TINY BELL, WE KNOW IT WELL. A
MAGIC BELL, IT KNOWS YOUR NAME - AND
WHERE YOU ARE — FROM WHERE YOU CAME. SO
KNOWING THIS IT SENDS TO YOU, A
CHRISTMAS WISH THAT'S OLD NOT NEW — FOR
HAPPY DAYS, FOR LOVE FOR HEALTH, FOR
ALL THAT'S GOOD, FOR YOU TRUE WEALTH
IT'S A LITTLE LIKE TINKER BELL —
YOU HAVE TO BELIEVE, BUT IF YOU LISTEN
WITH YOUR HEART YOU'LL HEAR IT —
AND MAY THE TINKLE OF A SMALL BELL
TELL YOU THAT WE HAVE YOU IN OUR HEARTS.

May 1979

Report on Clara Hilo Hattie Nelson.

Since the last report of December 1978 Clara's condition has remained stable. There have been no new problems and the old ones have remained under control. Although I realize that many of you have hope far beyond this, when we remember her age, her general physical condition, and the one massive stroke followed by a lesser one, we have to feel that where we are is the best that we can hope for.

In this book there is a choice collection of pictures of Clara, but there is one missing and it is truly a beauty. In January a liver scan by a nuclear camera showed that the lesion in the liver was substantially smaller than it has been eight months earlier!

The pictures that you do see are result of great amount of searching and probing by Milly Singletary. She has tackled every place and person who possibly might have information on Clara. While her searching has surfaced things that are new to me, there has been no dancing by skeletal bones in the closet. Clara's life has been a pleasure and only a pleasure to those who know her. A very few refused to be interviewed and the scanty or missing records in some places were something of a puzzle.

Here is Kaawa we are living comfortably with nothing of the institutional about Clara's care—our location is beautiful, our house cheerful, and the yard a mass of greenery and flowers. (While our papaya crop is not up to standard our chili pepper crop is bountiful.) Clara has all that affection and medical care and effort can provide.

Sadness of course. I sit here writing in the patio with the sound of the surf covering most sounds except the conversation of birds. Clara sleeps, as she does much of the time—medication is heavy and it has to be—without it she could not live. Sounds. Conversation. We never did really chatter much but there was always talk of even the most trivial happenings. Hope that she would regain the ability to speak really died hard. She has a few words, often misplaced, but very few in number. Can you picture Hilo Hattie of the robust and resonant voice unable to talk? I try to verbalize the daily happenings hoping that they will be of some interest to her even though I realize that her comprehension is limited.

Sadness of course. It ain't fair, that's all, it just ain't fair.

But again my love to you who love Clara. Carlyle

TOMORROW?

My first real concerns about tomorrow began about two years before the stroke when I would often consider our lives at that time and wonder, was I living in a fools paradise? While they were the best of years I can see now that I was trying to not recognize that Clara was slowly losing strength.

Even now that age has taken its toll on both of us I really do try to make the best of it. Clara's "Everything is for the best," has never come naturally to me but I shall live with it and I shall try to look at it with her eyes, those beautiful brown Hawaiian eyes.

Carlyle

Golf, needlepoint, making rugs—there are many sides to Clara's talents and she loves all pets. (Carlyle Nelson)

chapter twenty-six

The Other Side of Clara

Clara, the entertainer, is a legend in millions of homes throughout the land, but this many faceted lady is many other things, too.

Her talents in cooking have been explored in another chapter, but there's no question this phase of Clara's life has affected many people. During years of travel on the road she often created a meal reminiscent of Hawai‘i. Other times, it might be a big pot of her famous baked beans for a potluck lū‘au. When she was home, Clara often spent hours experimenting in gourmet cooking. Cooking recipes from newspapers, magazines, and friends are just another phase of that good life.

Back during the days when Clara was teaching school, bridge was another of her fun pastimes. After she quit teaching and went into entertaining full time, bridge took a back seat, although she constantly read the bridge columns, keeping up on what was new. Card playing during the entertainment years was usually confined to playing poker with the boys.

On the sporting scene, golf was her favorite activity. Inspired by sister Thelma, a tennis champ and golf enthusiast, Clara first took golf lessons while on the road. Several members of the troupe played golf and seemed to enjoy it very much. At first, Clara just tagged along to enjoy the fresh air and beautiful scenery. Finally, she decided to take lessons. After about four months, Thelma received a letter from Clara saying, "I shot eighty-two today." "Eighty-two?" Thelma pondered. "I've been playing for ten years and I don't always make eighty-two." Many years later, Thelma learned that Clara had been referring to nine holes. The golf game continued to be part of Clara's life until her mastectomy in 1966. Carlyle enjoyed the game too, and oftentimes they would just make a twosome on a beautiful bright Hawaiian day. Usually, Clara preferred walking to taking a cart.

Non-swimming was perhaps the most non-Hawaiian phase of Clara's life. She just didn't care for the water and never went swimming—couldn't swim, as a matter of fact. Even a dip in a pool on a hot day while they were traveling would be a rare event. Clara used to make quite a joke of it. "Did you ever hear of a pure Hawaiian that couldn't swim? That's me!"

All of the beautiful handicrafts were a natural for Clara. In the Thirties, when angora sweaters were the vogue, Clara would whip one up in no time. Lily Padeken Wai received one of those sweaters while they were working together at the St. Regis Hotel in New York. "I cherished it so much, I still have it today. Clara could knit in the dark. Sometimes, we'd go to a movie and Clara would sit there in the dark, watching the movie and knitting."

Crocheting, needlepoint, crewel, rug making—all were part of the handicraft scene for Clara. Once she made a rug for George Brent's secretary. It was about 8 x 10 feet and so heavy it took two men to carry it.

Gardening was another of Clara's favorite hobbies. "Wherever we lived," said Carlyle, "Clara would always have flowers growing. After we bought our home in Ka'a'awa, we had more ground to work with and Clara would experiment with a few vegetables—mostly lettuce and things like that. But first there were flowers. Always, when she tired of working in the garden, she would come in the house and start working on a rug or needlepoint."

That other side of Clara certainly should reflect a little on Clara's health.

"Clara has always been extremely healthy," Carlyle reports. "Never even has headaches. Her first major health blow came with the discovery of cancer in October of 1966."

Even that Clara took lightly. In a routine examination, the doctor found a lump in the left breast and advised a biopsy. Clara had told the doctor prior to going into surgery for the biopsy—"If you find anything wrong, yank it out. I trust you."

Carlyle remembers the day they went to the hospital. "She was her usual gay and cheerful self. We went to a Chinese restaurant and had chop sui for lunch, then checked her into the hospital. First thing Clara said when she came out of the anesthetic and was told about the operation, 'Oh, now they can call me Twiggy. I always wanted to look like her.'"

Clara's stay in the hospital was brief. Carlyle took her home to Ka'a'awa and took over as nurse, changing the dressings and performing other routine duties.

Serious as the operation was, it didn't affect her act, perhaps with one exception. No longer could she use her mythical horse, Kiele. It was just too heavy and too hard to get into. The only other major change in Clara's life was the necessity for a short haircut. Try as Carlyle would, he just couldn't comb that hair without pulling. "Ouch," Clara would say. So off came the long hair, and a new short bob was created.

The short hair affected only one number—the famous *Shinano Yoru*. No longer could she put up her hair like a geisha, sticking it with drumsticks, or whatever device she could lay her hands on. That made it necessary to buy a wig—but that turned out to be a plus item on the show. Clara bought one of those beautiful black Japanese hairdos like the real geishas wear and it really added to the act.

Later, her doctor found a lump in the right breast. While Clara was receiving anesthesia for the biopsy, her heart stopped. Naturally, all attention was diverted to her heart, with the result that a pacemaker was installed. Later, they performed the biopsy on the right breast, but it was found to be non-malignant.

The American Cancer Society has committees on various levels, a very active one being the Service and Rehabilitation Program that includes a service program called Reach to Recovery. It is a worldwide organization of women who have had mastectomies, and it is designed so each could help another recover mentally and physically.

In May of 1976, Reach to Recovery held a fashion show on the Oceania Restaurant in Honolulu, with all the models being mastectomies. The show was a huge success and the beautiful models certainly showed no signs of being "different."

Entertainment for the show included Hilo Hattie. The Cancer Society thought she would do two or three numbers, but to the audience's delight, she entertained for thirty to forty minutes. Song and dance were interspersed with Clara telling her own experience as a mastectomy. It was an inspirational speech.

"You can do a lot for yourself," Clara said. "Your attitude is important. But not only is YOUR attitude important, it's the attitude of the men in your life. I call them, the men, mastecto-men. And you (speaking to the men in the audience) can make or break a woman's spirit by your attitude. You have the privilege of allowing her to still feel like a woman, or completely ruin the relationship altogether. You—the mastecto-men—must weigh that choice."

Carlyle had been invited to make a world tour with the Madrigal Singers from Kailua under the direction of Shigeru Hotoke. In June of 1977, Clara and Carlyle boarded the S.S. *Monterey* for San Francisco. Clara did not want to go on the world tour, but thought she would spend some time on the Mainland visiting friends, then come home to Hawai'i and relax. The Madrigals' first appearance when they arrived on the Mainland was in Palo Alto at a special dinner honoring retiring members of the Palo Alto School District.

"I asked Clara if she would do a number," said Shigeru, "and she refused. This was so unlike Clara. I thought it strange, because I never heard Clara refuse before. She did agree to come up on stage and give out lei to the retirees, telling a few jokes, of course. The audience loved her. Later, when I heard about her stroke, I remember this incident and thought she must have not have been feeling well then."

Clara was staying with some dear friends, Allan and Betty Hunt, in Santa Clara. They had driven down to San Juan Baptista—that's the largest of the missions in the chain. Clara loved that area. She said she felt like Father Junipero Serra because she was walking on the same ground he had walked on. "From there we drove to Santa Cruz," Allan

Clara, herself a mastectomee, entertains at a fashion show with mastectomee models, and tells the mastecto-men how important their attitude is. (Cancer Society)

reports. “Clara always loved it at our Santa Cruz house. It is on a cliff overlooking the ocean and the surfers were out. She always said it reminded her of Hawai‘i. We just stayed there a short time and drove back home to Santa Clara.

“At Santa Clara, Betty had decorated our bathroom with a silk screen on foil which reads, ‘Heed not tomorrow, heed not yesterday. The magic words are here and now.’ Clara said that was her philosophy and the philosophy of all Hawaiians because they just loved life and lived it for the moment. We were sitting around the fireplace, talking. I finally excused myself, saying I was pooped from driving all day and I went to bed.

“Pretty soon, my wife came in, saying something had happened to Clara—she needed help. I jumped up and went into the living room. Sure enough, she was desperate for help. I dialed 911 and an ambulance was there within five minutes. They rushed her to O’Connors Hospital in San Jose. Clara had suffered a stroke.

“The problem now was to get in touch with Carlyle. He was scheduled to leave for overseas that very day with the Madrigals. I immediately called June Shipstad in Atherton. She was also a very good friend of Clara and Carlyle. Between them, they finally reached Carlyle just as he was about to board the plane.”

Clara’s illness is reported in more detail in the chapter entitled, “Carlyle Reminisces.”

Even through all that, the pacemaker held up very well until late 1978. Clara wasn’t feeling well and was having trouble breathing. Carlyle took her to see Dr. Lee at St. Francis Hospital in Honolulu. Liquid was found in her lungs, caused by the heart condition. In this modern age, they have a special medication for this condition and the liquid was eliminated and hasn’t recurred since.

Clara Inter as Hilo Hattie performing the *Hilo Hop.* (Bishop Museum)

The Ali'i float, Hilo's Merrie Monarch Festival in 1971. (Jack Lord)

First row (left to right): Marie and Jack Lord, Hilo Hattie, King Robert Kaiu Lindsey, and his wife Queen Leilehua Lindsey.

Second row (left to right): Auntie Violet Nathaniel, the late 'Iolani Lauhine (hidden behind Hilo Hattie), and the late Auntie Elizabeth Young.

chapter twenty-seven

Clara Remembers Hilo—Largest City on the Big Island

No book on Hilo Hattie would be complete unless we helped eliminate the myth that Clara was born in Hilo. As Clara remembers, "I've seen it in newspapers. I've even been asked if Haili Street was named for me. (That's my maiden name.) I've even had the same question about the Haili Church and that was built in 1859 by Protestant Missionaries.

"Hilo is a beautiful city, and indeed I would have been proud to have been born there, but the great Kahuna decided I should be born in Honolulu."

Clara's first trip to Hilo was in 1915 when she went to sing with her church choir. There have been many trips since—often to join in their many celebrations.

Hilo's largest celebration is the Merrie Monarch Festival scheduled the first week after Easter. The idea for a great festival, honoring King David Kalākaua, was conceived in 1963 by George Naope and Gene Wilhelm, and had its premiere in April of 1964. Each year the Mayor issues a proclamation:

> Whereas, this festival is for the purpose of recapturing the spirit which prevailed under the reign of King David Kalākaua, 1874–1891, through pageants, dancing and other activities; and whereas, such a festival will display some of our customs and spirits of old Hawaiʻi for the benefit of residents and visitors…

In 1969 the Festival was in danger of being eliminated for lack of a chairman when Dorothy Thompson of the Parks and Recreation Department volunteered to accept the job.

And what a job she did. The Merrie Monarch Festival grew so dramatically it is now known nationwide as one of the four top festivals of the year. Extra planes are flown in—hotels are bursting at the seams. The Hawai'i Visitors Bureau reports that at least 10,000 people visit the festival, particularly the last two days, which cover the famous hula contests.

In 1971, Clara was asked to be Honoree for the entire festival. Here's how she remembers it:

"I was Honoree that year, and what a ball I had. From the time I arrived Tuesday night until I left Sunday night, all Hilo seemed to be one big party. Wednesday morning they had me arrive at Mo'oheau Park in a helicopter. The keiki had a special program planned. There were children of all ages performing. Several of the high school girls asked me for my autograph and I was thrilled to think they knew of me. The festival committee even had a chauffeured limousine whisk me from one event to another. I was so happy. I would have been glad to ride my horse, Kiele, but he may have been too slow for that crowd.

"The official ceremony opened at Kūlana Na'auao with the traditional untwining of maile by then Mayor Shunichi Kimura, after a blessing from Reverend David Kaapu. The days were filled with hula shows, parades, pageants. Every day Ye Olde Grogge Shoppe would open, usually around three in the afternoon, and it would continue buzzing until late at night, always with live entertainment. In those days they had it in the Butler Building at the Civic Auditorium. Nowadays, they have it at the Seven Seas. In fact, in those days it was The Merry Monarch Festival. We didn't get so fancy with our spelling.

"The highlight of the event was the Royal Parade on Saturday afternoon. I got to ride on the Ali'i float with King and Queen, Robert Ka'iu Lindsey and his wife, Leilehua. Jack Lord was Grand Marshal that year, and he and his beautiful wife, Marie, were also on the float along with other celebrities as shown in the photograph at the beginning of this chapter."

Dorothy S. Thompson, Festival Chairman since 1969, remembers Clara's participation in the 1971 Merrie Monarch Festival with delight. "I have never met such a humble person. She said she was honored to be part of the festival, while we in turn felt honored to have her. When Clara walked into a room, everybody perked up. She's really number one. Everywhere she went, she performed. It didn't matter if it was in a shopping center, a bandstand, Ye Olde Grogge Shoppe—she was always ready, willing, and able to do a dance and sing a song. All who participated in the 1971 Merrie Monarch Festival will never forget the zest Hattie added to the event."

"That event was just one of the beautiful memories I have of Hilo, but I did want to set the record straight, that I was not born in Hilo."

Life is a funderful thing. (United Airlines, Jack O'Grady)

chapter twenty-eight

My Philosophy of Life

That other side of Clara must also reveal a more serious side as shown in her own handwriting. While Clara was cheerful and always had a gay salutation or a joke for the nurses and friends, the following words were written at Ka‘a‘awa after she was released from Kaiser for the supposed-to-be biopsy on the right breast, which resulted in the installation of the pacemaker in her heart.

"I was recently released from the hospital after what I try to relate as minor surgery. Our local gab columnist reported I was going in for a tune-up. I tried to keep it quiet but one thing led to another and before I knew it my room was filled with flowers and the mailman had his hands full. For which I was so grateful.

"Before entering the bedpan pavilion I kept remembering, or trying to, the lessons my mother had taught me—long ago. 'Do the best you can, and don't worry because everything happens for the best.' Well, I've done the best I can and it's darn difficult not to worry, but I'll go along with happening for the best. The best is an unknown factor because I do not fear death. I was not praying to live—I was requesting the 'Good Lord' to do whatever he wanted with my life. Had it turned out to be death, it would have been the best. Since it didn't, that was the best, and it's given me the opportunity I've wanted for a long time. I'm one that can put off day after day, but now I'm calling my own bluff and writing what I feel I must.

"So many people have asked me my philosophy on life—what my Hawaiian ancestry had to do with my beliefs, and how a woman can go on entertaining for as long as I have, still enjoy every minute of it, and get scared to death with each performance. To all who have known me, this book is dedicated. And to those who know me not, please read with an open mind and a kind heart.

"While occupying a lovely two-bed ward at the Royal Hawaiian Kaiser, I was fascinated and consumed with two wonderful books and, I believe, because of them, the urge has set my hand in motion. One was the popular Harold Robbins' book, 'The Pirate,' and the other was the best selling 'How To Be Your Own Best Friend,' by Drs. Mildred Newman and Bernard Berkowitz. As I finished 'The Pirate,' the last nine words sent thrills and put the stars in orbit."

'Isn't it true there is only one God?' (Last words are actually, "There is but one God.")

"But before I go on, may I ask you again to keep an open mind. I don't want 'God,' the word, to stop you. I use it only for convenience and quoting. If you have another word, use it, but I am referring to a greater element, a superior influence, a constant friend, our Father-Mother, the Great Omnipotent, but really, 'Isn't it true [that] there is only one God?' Many names and lots of idols, but only one Supreme Being.

"I refer to the two books that were given me, but let me say the Bible within the bedside table gave me many hours of pleasurable reading and introduced again to me the meaning of 'His' teachings and, especially, the word 'within.' It appears so many times and to all of us it's the only thing we can call our own. The only thing."

Clara certainly never believed in the hellfire and brimstone philosophy of religion. Many years ago Socrates said, "Know thyself." The same idea has been said in many ways—it's always new and always useful, no matter how many times it comes up in a new mu'umu'u. She has said many times and many ways, "I try to forget the past. Life is here and now."

Many years before Sophie Tucker made Mack Marauda's *Life is Just a Bowl of Cherries* popular, Mack offered it to Clara. She turned it down saying, "It isn't my style, my humor—and it isn't Hawaiian."

However, the words meant a lot to Clara and she used part of the lyrics many times in her closing program—"So live it and love it and make the most of it, cause life is a wonderful thing." She did say, many years later, that if she HAD recorded it, she would have coined the word, "funderful," for "wonderful." "Because life is a funderful thing."

There are many songs that meant a lot to Clara that were not in her repertoire. One of her favorites was the famous Lili'uokalani's Prayer (lyrics courtesy of Halekūlani Hotel) which the Queen wrote while imprisoned at 'Iolani Palace. We'd like to share the words with you:

LILI'UOKALANI'S PRAYER

'O kou aloha nō Aia i ka lani A 'o kou 'oia 'i'o He hemolele hō'i	Oh Lord thy loving mercy Is high as the heavens; It tells us of thy truth And 'tis filled with holiness.
Ko'u noho mihi 'ana A pā 'ahao 'ia 'O 'oe ku'u lama Kou nani ko'u ko'o	Whilst humbly meditating Within these walls imprisoned, Thou art my light my haven Thy glory my support.
Mai nānā 'ino 'ino Nā hewa o kānaka Akā e huikala A ma'ema'e nō	Oh! Look not on their failings, Nor on the sins of men Forgive with loving kindness That we might be made pure.
No laila e ka Haku Malalo o kou 'ēhou Kō mākou maluhia A mau loa aku nō. 'Āmene.	For thy grace I beseech Thee; Bring us 'neath Thy protection And peace will be our portion, Now and forever more. Amen.

For the millions of friends who have smiled and laughed because of Clara's antics, we all say "thank you." She is a beautiful example of the meaning of love—of the true aloha spirit. She was never too tired to do a little more for her fellow man—always happy to make others feel glad they are alive. The wonderment of her life—its every turn of events has culminated in the happiness of others. God truly blessed this beautiful woman with an ability and capacity for sharing and for caring, for giving and, sometimes, receiving. The world is a much better place because she has touched our lives. Her love and laughter will be with us always in so many wonderful ways.

How good is life—the sheer joy of being here—how wonderful to have all of the heart, soul, and senses forever in joy.

God Bless You, Clara Hilo Hattie Nelson. We love you too!

Index